THIS MAGNIFICENT SALVATION

What Salvation Means in a World Like This

A BAPTIST BELIEFS AND HERITAGE STUDY FOR LIFE TODAY

Duane Brooks

BAPTISTWAYPRESS®

Dallas, Texas

BAPTISTWAY PRESS® Management Team
Executive Director, Baptist General Convention of Texas: Randel Everett
Director, Education/Discipleship Center: Chris Liebrum
Director, Bible Study/Discipleship Team: Phil Miller
Publisher, BAPTISTWAY PRESS®: Ross West

Cover and Interior Design and Production: Desktop Miracles, Inc.
Printing: Data Reproductions Corporation

This book is produced in cooperation with the Baptist Distinctives Council/Texas Baptist Heritage Center of the Baptist General Convention of Texas—Executive Director Emeritus, BGCT, and volunteer Director, Texas Baptist Heritage Center, William M. Pinson, Jr.; volunteer Director of Organization and Communication, Doris Tinker.

First edition: January 2010
ISBN-13: 978-1-934731-47-5

To Melanie, wonderful wife,
marvelous mother to Graham, Chase, and Casey,
and perfect partner in ministry

About This Study

"It's crucial that we keep a firm grip on what we've heard so that we don't drift off. If the old message delivered by the angels was valid . . . do you think we can risk neglecting this latest message, this magnificent salvation?" (Hebrews 2:1–3, *The Message*).[1]

This book—*This Magnificent Salvation*—is one of a series of books on Baptist beliefs and heritage that BAPTISTWAY PRESS® is producing. These studies are intended both for individual reading and study and for group studies in churches and other settings.[2]

The intent of this series is to provide guidance in considering, understanding, and acting on some of our deeply-held Baptist beliefs, particularly as these beliefs intersect with current life. The intent is *not* to produce an official statement about these Baptist beliefs. Even to attempt to do so would go against the very nature of who Baptists are.

So, as you read and study this book and the other studies in the series, be prepared to think seriously and carefully. Engage the ideas with your own thought and study, especially of the Bible.

In addition to this study book, suggestions for teaching this study are available in *This Magnificent Salvation—Teaching Guide*, available at www.baptistwaypress.org. See www.baptistwaypress.org for additional resources for this and other studies produced by BAPTISTWAY PRESS®.

Table of Contents

The Writer: Duane Brooks

Duane Brooks is pastor of Tallowood Baptist Church, Houston, Texas. Dr. Brooks has served on the Executive Board and the Human Welfare Board of the Baptist General Convention of Texas and on the Board of Regents at Baylor University. He holds the Ph.D. from Baylor University. Duane was called to preach while in middle school in Germany and ordained in Great Falls, Montana. Duane has served as pastor in four Texas Baptist churches—Pleasant Grove in Rosebud, Williams Creek in Mart, New Hope in Cedar Park, and Tallowood in Houston. Duane and his wife Melanie have three children: Graham, Chase, and Casey.

One

A Mighty Savior

Old Testament Snapshots of Salvation

"The LORD your God . . . is mighty to save."

—ZEPHANIAH 3:17

WHY DID WESLEY AUTRY DO it? In a daring rescue, he amazed New York City. On January 2, 2007, Autry took his two daughters with him to ride the subway en route to school and work. As they waited for a train, a total stranger named Cameron Hollopeter apparently suffered an epileptic seizure and fell off the platform, landing on the subway track below.

Asking others to care for his girls, Autry jumped down on the tracks and tried to lift Hollopeter to safety. Unfortunately, the train was too close. As it closed in on them, Autry covered Hollopeter, wrapping his arms and legs up underneath while the train went over them.

After he saved Hollopeter's life, Autry made the talk show circuit as an instant celebrity. Donald Trump heard the story and gave Autry $10,000. Autry also received free tickets to take his daughters to Disney World.[1] Still, no one could account for Autry's extraordinary kindness at such great risk to himself. (I've been to Disney World, and I liked it. But I did not see anything about the place that would make me say, *OK, I will jump down on a railroad track in the subway.*) Of course, when Autry acted, he had no idea that he would receive any sort of compensation.

Autry's compassion to a stranger points to the grand narrative, the bigger story of the saving love of God. Can we see the parallels to Christ's sacrifice on the cross? The danger was real. Like us, Hollopeter possessed no ability or strength to save himself. Deliverance to safety involved enormous risk to the rescuer. One stark contrast reveals the limitation of the metaphor: Jesus not only risked his life but sacrificed it to save the world.

No wonder the Apostle Paul wrote, "I am not ashamed of the gospel, because it is the power of God for the salvation of everyone who believes: first for the Jew, then for the Gentile" (Romans 1:16–17). The story of God's saving work in the lives of human beings reaches its dramatic crescendo in the New Testament. But it does not begin there. The salvation story begins in the Old Testament. Unforgettable images of God as Savior emerge in metaphor, in music, and in prophecy. Salvation is the unforgettable story that God told, is telling, and will tell for eternity.

Beginning at the Beginning (Genesis)

Salvation begins at the beginning. Shortly after creation, humankind fell in sin. Adam and Eve, who had known such sweet fellowship with God, disobeyed God. Their choice led directly to isolation and shame. God sought them and found them. Even in God's pursuit of Adam and Eve, we catch a glimpse of the God who desires to save humankind. Presumably through the sacrifice of an animal, God provided a covering for the woman and the man (Genesis 3:21). Nevertheless, they were punished and removed from the garden, lest they also reach out and take the fruit from the tree of life (Gen. 3:22–24). God forgave them but also held them responsible for their choices.

Sin began with Adam and Eve and inevitably erupted again, disrupting the lives of all of their descendants. This drama unfolds before our eyes in the first eleven chapters of Genesis. Adam and Eve's son Cain killed his brother Abel in what might have been the very first worship war. Generations rose and fell with only an occasional reference to one like Enoch, who walked with God (Gen. 5:22–24).

In Noah's story we sense once again God's frustration with sin and see his punishment of all creation. But out of that devastation, God chose and redeemed a solitary family. Preserved in an ark, Noah trusted God to protect him from the flood (Gen. 6—8).

Later, humankind built a tower in Babel to reach up to God and "make a name for [them]selves" (Gen. 11:4). God responded to the builders in Babel by dispersing them across the earth. Pride led to their fall.

Have you noticed that history sometimes repeats itself? The human need to eclipse the work of others and exalt ourselves is still very much with us. Perhaps you have heard about a building under construction in Dubai called Burj Dubai. It reaches more than 800 meters (about 2,625 feet) into the air.[2] Engineers say it will be the tallest building ever built—so far. Likely the record will not stand long. Likely a taller one will be built.

Warning against greed, Jesus told of a man who tore down his barns to build bigger ones in celebration of his own self-centered success. Soon, he forfeited it all upon his death (Luke 12:16–21).

At the strategic moment in history after the incident of the tower of Babel, God started to move in the life of Abraham, who would be blessed and become a blessing (Genesis 12:1–3). God's blessing promised salvation to future generations through Abraham's descendant Jesus Christ. In the remainder of the Old Testament we find specific portraits of the God who is mighty to save accomplishing his great work of salvation and offering a harbinger of future hope. In the story of Moses, for example, we get a glimpse of the God who is mighty to save.

God, Our Delivering Savior (Exodus)

Whose number do you dial when you need help? Last year one of our teenaged sons called me for help because his car had a flat tire. Flattered by his confidence and seizing the teachable moment, I decided to show him how to change a tire. It turned into a disaster. The person who put the lug nuts on the wheel apparently had a better tool than I possessed to remove them. Still worse, the wheel would not budge even after I removed the lug nuts.

So I followed my son's example. I called my father, who, I am thankful to say, doubles as an outstanding mechanic. With dad on the phone and a large hammer in hand, we finally removed the tire from the car. Our victory celebration was interrupted by our discovery that the small spare we found in the trunk was also flat. My father, who lives for the moments when we need his help, coached us to air up the spare with a bicycle tire pump. All the while, my wife Melanie found it highly entertaining as we passed the phone back and forth and pumped up the tire for a very long while. Jokes about how many generations of the Brooks family it takes to change a tire began that very night.

When Israel needed help, the people called on the Lord. The Book of Exodus recounts the plight of their bondage in Egypt. A new pharaoh who did not know Joseph demanded they perform hard labor. When they cried out to the Lord, he saw, heard, cared, and sent a deliverer to save them.

One of the most important Old Testament words for salvation speaks of the sovereign rescue of men and nations. The word *yasha*, which means *to bring out into a spacious place*, also gives us the name *Yeshua*, the root of the names Joshua and later Jesus.[3] Nowhere do we see this concept more clearly than in the Old Testament story of the Exodus. When God's people cried for help, God came to their rescue and brought them out into a spacious place of their own in the Promised Land.

God Our Savior Sees! (Exod. 3:7)

It is easy to feel forgotten. Does God know we are here? Does God understand our situation? Does God care? The Exodus story answers with a resounding, *Yes!* God saw the people's need. The only question was whether Moses would see the God who was seeing him.

As the poet Elizabeth Barrett Browning put it,

> Earth's crammed with heaven,
> And every common bush afire with God;
> But only he who sees, takes off his shoes,
> The rest sit round it and pluck blackberries,
> And daub their natural faces unaware.[4]

On the whole, sheep require less maintenance than people. After Moses' first failed deliverance of the Israelites (Exod. 2:11–15), he grew comfortable tending sheep. After forty years perhaps, he would have been content for the rest of his life just to pasture and pastor his sheep.

But Moses found himself at Mount Horeb, "the mountain of God," with his sheep (Exod. 3:1). There he discovered in the wilderness Somebody who knew him by name. God came to him speaking from a burning bush. After Moses looked, saw the bush, stopped, and removed his shoes, we learn that God saw that Moses saw (Exod. 3:3–4). Perhaps, like other reclusive desert-dwellers, Moses did not particularly want to be seen by such a powerful Savior, and so he refused to look at God (Exod. 3:6). Then God revealed his intention to save, "I have indeed seen the misery of my people. . . . I have come down to rescue them" (Exod. 3:7–8). God identified himself to Moses as the Savior who would deliver the people and rescue them from oppression. This offers a marvelous portrait of the great God who loves and lives to save.

On that day Moses discovered that God had a greater and higher purpose for his life. In fact, God revealed to him a purpose that was worth the investment of the rest of his life. Have we found that purpose yet? What is worth the investment of our whole lives?

God said, *Moses, I have something for you to do.* When Moses implied that he would really rather not be involved, God said, "I will be with you" (Exod. 3:12). In effect, God reminded him, *This is not about you, Moses. This is not about your feelings. This is about my plan to rescue, redeem, and ransom my people.*

Powerfully, God revealed himself as the God who is both willing and able to save. God is in the saving business. In fact, God has a corner on the market of that business. God is the only Savior available; the only One who can rescue us from our inescapable dilemmas. God remains the only one who can lift us "out of the mud and mire" and "set [our] feet on a rock" (Psalm 40:2). He is the only God, our Savior. If we would believe it and receive it, God earnestly desires to save us. He is willing to save.

Have we yet seen the God who sees? We remember the slave girl Hagar's story in Genesis (Gen. 16). This slave girl, who was carrying Abram's child, was banished from the camp by Abram's wife Sarai. Fleeing, Hagar found herself alone in the wilderness. At least she thought she was alone. But even there God found her, and she gave God a new name. She said, "You are the God who sees me. . . . I have now seen the One who sees me" (Gen. 16:13). How about us? Have we seen the God who sees us?

God Our Savior Hears! (Exod. 3:7)

God not only sees. God also hears.

One of my college roommates, Mark Johnson, developed as a baritone soloist in the School of Music at Baylor University. He sang on occasion at Pleasant Grove Baptist Church near Rosebud, where I served as a student pastor. Every morning he awakened the dawn and our apartment as he warmed up to prepare his voice to sing. I can still hear the song he adapted from Psalm 116. "I love the Lord, because he hears my prayers and answers them, because he bends down and listens. And I will praise him as long as I live."

Our God is the God who both sees and hears. "I have heard them crying out because of their slave drivers" (Exod. 3:7). We may wrongly suppose we are alone in our sorrow. Lest we think nobody knows when we are crying in the darkness, God has always heard our cries for help. He is the God who hears us well and understands.

In fact, our hearing problem stems not from God's inability to hear us, but from our inability to hear him. Isn't this why Jesus would later say, "He who has ears, let him hear"? (Matthew 11:15).

As disciples, we learn to listen closely like Elijah on the mountain (1 Kings 19:9–18). When the rushing of the wind, the rumble of the earthquake, and the roar of the fire ceased, then Elijah heard God's still, small voice. Similarly, in our turbulent world, over the cacophony of sounds around us, and above all the voices clamoring to be heard, there is only one voice we must hear. Like Elijah, Moses heard God call him by name. Have we heard that voice? Have we, like Isaiah, cultivated the ear of a disciple (Isaiah 50:4–5)?[5] Our God is the God who speaks. If we will listen, we will hear.

Have you heard of the *mosquito ringtone?* Our young students at our church know this subtle sound. At 17 kilohertz high, the tone is a very high pitched, almost squealing sound, imperceptible to those of us over the age of twenty-five or so. Younger people, however, hear the *mosquito tone* well. Supposedly, it was invented by an enterprising businessman in England who was trying to disperse a group of teenagers loitering around his business. Alas, the displaced teens laughed last. Not without recourse, teenagers in many places have turned the tables, choosing the largely inaudible tone as the ringtone for their own phones, thus eluding the detection of many of their parents and teachers.

How did I learn about it? Without my knowledge, during a recent sermon, one of our young sound technicians, Miguel Ortiz, played the *mosquito tone* over the sound system to illustrate my point. Unaware of his actions, I looked around the room and noticed the students were all covering their ears while I was preaching. This was likely not the first time they had wanted to do this, but I was puzzled by their honesty. Meanwhile, most of the adults listened to the sermon, unaware of the tone. Anatomically speaking, students can still hear it because they still have the microscopic hairs in their ears that enable them to detect it. As we grow older, these hairs diminish and deteriorate, depriving us of the ability to hear higher-pitched noises.

Voluntarily, we sometimes surrender the ability to hear the still, small voice of God. Does this happen because we are tuned in to every other frequency except the tone of our Father's voice? Do we still hear the God who hears our cries? The news gets better. Because our God hears, he also cares.

God Our Savior Cares

"I am concerned about their suffering" (Exod. 3:7). God showed compassion to the Israelites when they languished under the oppression of the Egyptians. We must be careful to note that this is not an indictment against all of Egypt for all time.[6] Instead this story relates to a particular time period of great oppression in Egypt. God had used Joseph's captivity to preserve Jacob and his family during a time of famine.

Centuries later, a pharaoh emerged who did not know the story of Joseph or the original host and guest relationship (Exod. 1:8). Unfortunately, the relationship had changed, with the Egyptians becoming masters and the Israelites slaves. In this incredibly dark time, God expressed his concern from a burning bush. God our unchanging Savior still cares. As God cared about the oppression of the Israelites, God cares about us. Even now, God cares for the last, the lost, and the least in this world more than we can comprehend. In the New Testament, Peter reminds us, "Cast all your anxiety on him because he cares for you" (1 Peter 5:7). There is still "a wideness in God's mercy."[7]

God's love extends well beyond our own concern for others. In the Old Testament Book of Jonah, the prophet expressed little concern for the Ninevites when God told him to go to Nineveh and proclaim God's message so that they might repent. Hearing of a similar need, the prophet Isaiah had offered, "Here am I. Send me!" (Isaiah 6:8). By fleeing the opposite direction, Jonah said, in effect, *I am not here. Send somebody else.* En route to Tarshish, God sent him a *whale-o-gram* and garnered his undivided attention (Jonah 1:17). There Jonah repented. After he was spared and delivered to the shore, he decided to obey, although he did so grudgingly. One suspects that Jonah really hoped the Ninevites would not repent so that they would be destroyed. After preaching, he took a front row seat on the east side of the city just to watch the fireworks as God destroyed the city (Jonah 4:5).

Jonah was a better preacher than he knew or wanted to be. The people of Nineveh, following their king, responded with surprising repentance. Imagine Jonah's shock when God saw their repentance and relented of sending calamity on Nineveh. It burned Jonah that Nineveh was not burned.

To teach Jonah a lesson in compassion, God graciously appointed a vine to grow up and give him shade. Jonah loved that vine. Later, God appointed a worm to destroy it. As the vine fell, so did Jonah's countenance. Some of us understand better than others that there is no sunburn like a sunburn on one's head.

God asked Jonah the same question he asks us when we get angry: "Have you any right to be angry?" (Jonah 4:4). When Jonah defended his anger, God indicted him,

> *You have been concerned about this vine, though you did not tend it or make it grow. It sprang up overnight and died overnight. But Nineveh has more than a hundred and twenty thousand people who cannot tell their right hand from their left, and many cattle as well. Should I not be concerned about that great city? (Jonah 4:10–11).*

God cares. This is how we know our God. He is the God who cares, who is willing to save—indeed, who desires to save all people.

God Our Savior Comes to Us

How much does God care? He cares enough to send the very best. In Exodus 3:8 God said, "I have come down to rescue them. . . ." This story foreshadows the incarnation and first coming of Christ. Similar to what Wesley Autry, the subway hero, did, our God dives in and delivers us. "The Word became flesh and made his dwelling among us" (John 1:14). "God so loved that he gave his only Son" to come into the world (John 3:16). Once again we see God taking the initiative. Salvation belongs to our God!

We celebrate our God's willingness and ability to save. He comes down to rescue. The Exodus account strongly implies that God plans to succeed. When Moses gave all kinds of excuses, God made it clear that he knew Pharaoh and had a plan. God said, in effect, *I know how powerful Pharaoh is, but when this is all over, Pharaoh will know how powerful I am. He will know that I am with you. I am mighty to save.* God promised to lift the Israelites up and out of this bondage. Can you believe it? God wants to deliver us even more than we want to be delivered.

Later the Israelites lamented leaving Egypt at all. They preferred slavery in Egypt to freedom in their own land.

Ian McConnell was one of the pilots who flew the helicopters into New Orleans on August 30, 2005, when the levee broke after Hurricane Katrina came. In his first three missions, he safely delivered eighty-nine people, three dogs, and one cat out of windows and from rooftops. Still, he remembered the fourth mission best. Why? On that trip he delivered nobody. Unfortunately, the people decided to stay and take their chances there, not knowing how desperate their situation was.[8] If only they had known that their only chance of deliverance had come, they would have gone willingly and gratefully.

This idea may well explain the reticence of some to trust God to save. Perhaps we do not know how desperate our situation is. *Status quo* is just another way of saying *the mess we are in.* Our desperate situation calls for a deliverer, a savior, one who can rescue us. God wanted to bring the Israelites out of Egypt.

Not only did God save them *from* something. God also saved them *for* something and *to* something. God explained, *I want to take them back to this mountain so they can worship me* (Exod. 3:12). Early in the story we learn what God wants for us: worship. Intimacy with God is better than any other thing God gives to us. To know God and be known by God exceeds by far God's other gifts in this world.

Not only did the Israelites leave their Egyptian bondage, but they came into a spacious land, fulfilling the word *yasha,* which means *to come into an accommodating space, to have breathing room, to be free of captivity and bondage.* Jesus asked the lame man by the pool of Bethesda, "Do you want to get well?" (John 5:6). Literally Jesus inquired, *Do you want to be made whole and complete?* This remains God's question today. If we will receive it, our God not only rescues but also redeems.

God as Kinsman Redeemer (Ruth)

When I think I have had a bad day, I remember James. James grew up in our extended family after his mom died of an aneurysm on the night he was born. Early in his life, James was raised by his dad, who remarried after his mom's death. His parents and grandparents loved him greatly. Tragically, before James reached the age of twelve, both his dad and his step-mom died. One of my brothers and his wife raised James in their home, taking him to one of our Texas Baptist churches. There James experienced love and grew as a disciple. Recently, while in his early twenties, he was killed by a drunk driver. Our family wondered, when all of life caves in, what then? We may wonder aloud in times like this: *Is God there? Does God care?* Pastor Jeff Warren's sermon at James's funeral confirmed God's compassion to our whole family. God gave our family the chance to know and love James for the season we shared. Even that tragedy is redeemed by the promise of eternal life. Having endured multiple tragedies, Ruth and Naomi may have wondered also, but they found a redeemer.

God saves us by redeeming us. The Hebrew language offers us a number of words that speak of redemption. One is the word *goel,* which speaks of a kinsman who redeems.[9] The classic example of the kinsman-redeemer is the love story of Boaz and Ruth. Their love story started in the biblical time period of the Judges. In a season of great famine, a man named Elimelech took his wife Naomi and his sons Mahlon and Kilion, left Bethlehem, and moved over across the Jordan to Moab. There the sons broke God's covenant by intermarrying with the Moabites, who worshiped different gods. Mahlon and Kilion married Orpah and Ruth, respectively.

Then things became worse when Elimelech, the father, died. Not long afterward, Naomi's sons both died, leaving three widows in Moab. Naomi decided to go home, but she didn't want to take her Moabite daughters-in-law with her, thinking their best chances for remarriage and survival were in their own country. Taking the opportunity, Orpah stayed, but Ruth would not. We remember her extraordinary words of devotion:

*Don't urge me to leave you or to turn back from you. Where you go, I
will go and where you stay I will stay. Your people will be my people and
your God my God. Where you die I will die and there I will be buried.
May the lord deal with me be it ever so severely if anything but death
separates you and me (Ruth 1:17).*

Naomi and Ruth returned to Bethlehem. When her relatives
saw Naomi, they were glad to see her, but she was bitter. She said,
"Don't call me Naomi. Call me Mara because the Almighty has made
my life very bitter" (Ruth 1:20). Clearly, she was grieving the loss of
her family. But things were about to change. The barley harvest had
begun. Ruth went to the field to pick up the leftovers—to glean after
the workers harvested. While there the Lord smiled on her, and grace
transformed her great grief into great joy.

You have heard of Murphy's law? *Everything that can go wrong, will go
wrong.* Ruth might have considered Murphy an optimist. First, Ruth
was a young widow in a time when a single woman was defenseless
and helpless, without rights or income. Second, Ruth had no children.
In the Old Testament, children often served as an asset rather than
a financial liability. In Ruth's case, when they were grown up, they
would have helped to support their mother. Third, Ruth lived in a foreign land where she had no rights at all. The Israelites did not look
with favor on the Moabites.[10] In some cases, a foreign woman turned
to prostitution for survival. Ruth had three strikes against her.

Nearly everything that could have gone wrong in Ruth's life at
this point had gone wrong, but things were about to change. God's
law trumps Murphy's law. Paul captured this in his letter to the
Romans. He wrote, "And we know that in all things God works for
the good of those who love him, who have been called according to
his purpose" (Romans 8:28).

When everything had gone wrong, the one Person who could
help Ruth was working actively for her welfare. Even though Ruth
was totally incapable of saving or helping herself, Someone was looking out for her. Out of all the fields in Bethlehem, when she went out
to work, she happened to choose the one owned by Boaz, a relative of
her husband's family.

First among Boaz's amazing credentials was his personal knowledge of the Lord. He knew the Lord, and he blessed others in the name of the Lord, trusting God's providence in his own life and Ruth's (Ruth 2:4, 12). Boaz was all about God. If we ever find anyone who has a heart for God, we should knit our souls to that person.

We counsel our young people at Tallowood Baptist Church that at the top of the list of qualities they look for in a mate, they should seek this one first: a heart for God. Once one determines to seek a person with a heart for God, then nobody else need even apply for the job.

Boaz talked a lot about God, but how do we know he really knew the Lord? We see it in the way he treated people—his employees and Ruth, a stranger in Israel.

After 9/11 in the United States, we have witnessed considerable *xenophobia*—literally *fear of foreigners* but in many cases *dislike of foreigners*. We may be sure of this: when we are kind to a stranger and help a helpless person from another country, we are very near to the heart of our God. God has welcomed Gentiles like us into his family.

We marvel at the way Boaz provided food for Ruth (Ruth 2:8, 16) and protected her (Ruth 2:9, 22). The law of the Old Testament was to be kind to strangers, but foreigners, especially young single servant girls, were often abused. Thankfully, Boaz protected her from harm, not allowing others to take advantage of her. We also learn that Boaz cared enough about her to know her story (Ruth 2:11). She wondered at his grace, "Why have I found such favor in your eyes that you notice me—a foreigner?" (Ruth 2:10). He talked to her and invited her to eat with him.

Ultimately, Boaz became her kinsman-redeemer. In Israel if a man died, a close family member could buy his land. The law also required him to take the widow as his wife, knowing that the children born would belong to the deceased. This law kept a person's family lineage alive if he died. Recognizing this possibility, Naomi sent Ruth to lie at the feet of Boaz on the threshing floor. When Boaz woke up, she proposed marriage to him by putting the corner of his blanket over herself. Depicted in Hollywood, this story might have become steamy, but Boaz lived with integrity. Because Ruth was not his wife, he carefully protected her and her reputation (Ruth 3:13–15). One other kinsman had a prior claim, but that kinsman refused his right to redeem.

Ruth's love story is a story of grace. Boaz, for no apparent reason, showed kindness to her as her kinsman redeemer, agreeing to purchase her land and also to marry her. Our salvation love story with God is also a story filled with grace. We are empty without God, but God makes our lives full. We do not choose God, but God chooses us, loves us, and saves us. Our God is, has always been, and always will be the God who is mighty to save.

Love does not balk at the cost. Given the chance, Boaz redeemed Ruth because he was willing to marry her, no matter what it cost him.

As a boy, Chiune Sugihara dreamed of becoming Japan's ambassador to Russia. By the 1930s, as ambassador to Lithuania, he was a step away from fulfilling his dream. One morning a huge throng gathered outside his home. Sugihara learned they were Jews who had fled there from Poland, seeking Sugihara's help for Japanese visas that would permit them to escape the German Gestapo. Three times Sugihara wired Tokyo for permission to provide the visas; three times his request was rejected. Sugihara, a committed Christian, had to choose between his dream and the lives of the crowd. Sugihara chose to disobey orders. For the next twenty-eight days, he wrote visas by hand, barely sleeping or eating. Recalled to Berlin, he departed still writing visas and shoving them through the train window into the hands of refugees running alongside. Ultimately his work saved 6,000 lives.

Back in Japan, Sugihara's remaining days were spent selling light bulbs. When his story was finally told, his son was asked, "How did your father feel about his choice?" His answer surprises, "My father's life was fulfilled. When God needed him to do the right thing, he was available to do it."[11]

What did Jesus give up to redeem us? Everything. He paid a high price to purchase our souls.

Given the chance, God redeemed us. Like Ruth, we are trophies of grace. Ruth later became the great-grandmother of the great King. This is a great love story. Is it ours? Can you believe God redeems us and makes us God's own?

God as Redeemer of Our Rebellion (Hosea)

Did you hear about the man who wanted his kidney back? A Long Island, New York, surgeon embroiled in a divorce proceeding wanted his estranged wife to return the kidney he donated to her, although he says he'll settle for $1.5 million in compensation.[12] The surgeon said he decided to go public with his demand for kidney compensation because he had grown frustrated with the negotiations with his estranged wife. Dr. Batista fought back tears after talking about a bitter divorce battle he's embroiled in with his estranged wife. Apparently, he gave his kidney to his wife and afterward accused her of infidelity.

Whether or not his allegations are true, the story raises a question: If someone saved your life, could you ever be unfaithful to that person? Just as unfaithfulness frequently makes the news today, God's people proved unfaithful to him again and again.

Another Old Testament word for salvation is *padah,* which means *to redeem by giving something in exchange.*[13] An example emerges from the story of the Old Testament prophet Hosea.

A preacher named Hosea in the Northern Kingdom of Israel received a word from God telling him to marry Gomer, a woman who had a rather poor reputation. We can imagine that she lived up to the meaning of *Gomer,* her name, which means *beautiful.* Perhaps for a season, their union was beautiful. Over time, Gomer began to stray, eventually leaving Hosea altogether.[14] God sent Hosea to find her. Hosea's personal story mirrored the story of God and the Israelites. As Hosea married Gomer, and then lost her to unfaithfulness, so God loved Israel, but Israel pursued other gods.

Unquestionably, God has been faithful to us. We sing, "Great is Thy faithfulness, Lord, unto me!"[15] What if we changed the pronouns? Could we sing to God, "Great is [our] faithfulness, Lord unto [you]"? The real question is, *Have we been faithful to God? Have we loved anyone or anything more than we love God?* Like Gomer, we sometimes rebel and run from God's love. What if we walk away from God? Will God stop loving us? No. God has redeemed us with something more precious than silver and barley (see Hosea 3:2). He bought us with the precious blood of his only Son. Our God answers our rebellion with redemption!

Like Hosea, God redeems his people and brings us back to himself. God pleaded with Israel to return to him. He agonized over their sinful choices. Sometimes we think of our sin and skip immediately to the forgiveness. But Hosea reminds us of God's anguish over sin. Even so, God says to those who are not his own, you are loved; you are my people (Hosea 2:23).

The Lord told Hosea to go and love his wife again. Years ago, my pastor Larry Nixon interpreted these verses in a powerful sermon. After Gomer left Hosea, she came back through the town on an auction block. At first, Hosea bid pieces of silver, all the money he had, but it was not enough. So he added to his bid a homer and a half of barley, perhaps all the food they had left in the house (Hosea 3:2). He gave everything he had to buy his wife back out of adultery. The Book of Hosea shows us God's redemptive love for us.

In Paul's Letter to the Romans, Paul told our story in similar terms, "God commends his love toward us in this: While we were still sinners, Christ died for us" (Rom. 5:8). In our story of salvation: it is not our love for God that brought us to him, but God's love for us!

This divine love draws us inexorably to God. Will we return to God? "Sow for yourselves righteousness; reap the fruit of unfailing love, and break up your unplowed ground; for it is time to seek the LORD until he comes and showers righteousness on you" (Hosea 10:12).

This Amazing Story

I once heard an amazing story of redemption. Years ago during wartime, an American went to a foreign country on assignment, leaving his wife behind. For a period of time, he wrote and declared his love for her. Then one day the letters stopped coming. After a while, the wife's worst fears were realized. Her husband had fallen in love with a woman in the other country. He would not be coming home after all. His wife was heartbroken. Sometime later, word came that he had died there. A strange letter bearing an unthinkable request followed in the mail. The woman her husband had loved in the other country had borne two children to him. Would she, the forsaken wife, bring them to the United States so they could escape the ravages of war? Amazingly, the wife brought them. This is redeeming love, like the love of the heavenly Father. What would we do if someone loved us like that? Wouldn't we love in return?

These amazing words and stories of salvation remind us that our God is our Savior, our Kinsman-Redeemer and the Lover who remains faithful even when we are not. From the beginning our Lord has always been the God who saves.

A pastor at my ordination at Westside Baptist Church in Great Falls, Montana, prayed with these unforgettable words, "Lord, you are a great God and a mighty Savior." He was right. This is good news for us, because more than anything, we need a Savior. In the next chapter we'll discover the reason.

CHAPTER *Two*

We Need a Savior

"For all have sinned and fall short
of the glory of God. . . ."

—ROMANS 3:23

WE CAN NEVER BE SAVED until we know we have sinned. There's a great story about a mom who lived with her children in an apartment complex. The children played hide and seek on a hot summer day. Roofers had left empty tar barrels in the parking lot. The youngest of the children spied an opportunity and hid in one of the empty barrels. He won the game but lost the war, because he was covered with smudges of tar when he emerged from the barrel. At arm's length, his eldest brother led him to the door and called for mom. She came to the door, eyed the boy from head to foot, and said, "Son, I declare, it would be easier to make another one than to clean you up."

We could understand if our Creator sometimes felt that way about us. Left to our own devices, we make a mess of things.

Our recognition of our sinfulness is the first step toward finding salvation. Frequently, parents ask me, *How will I know when my child is prepared to receive Christ as Savior?* I always answer, *We cannot be saved until we know we have sinned.*

The theologian William Temple put it even more pointedly, "the only thing of my very own which I contribute to my redemption is the sin from which I need to be redeemed."[1] We need a Savior.

Sin Defined: Overviewing Our Problem with Sin

What exactly is sin? A number of words for sin emerge from our study of the Bible. One common word in the Greek New Testament is *hamartanein*, which means *to miss the mark*. A second Greek word for sin is *parabainein*, which means *to trespass or cross boundaries*. Still another word, *paraptoma,* means *to turn aside*.[2] A fourth term from the Hebrew Old Testament can be translated *rebellion*, which results in *separation from fellowship with God*.[3]

Theologians sometimes distinguish between *sin* and *sins*.[4] *Sin*, when not referring to one specific sin, refers to the sinful nature, enslaving principle, or power that controls sinners. On the other hand, the term *sins* in the plural speaks of the specific choices people make.[5] By one count, the New Testament identifies sinful behavior with at least 115 different words.[6] Our propensity to sin is captured in this line from a hymn, "Prone to wander, Lord, I feel it, Prone to leave the God I love."[7]

Baptist theologian W. T. Conner explained our need for the term *sin*, "Crime is against the state. Immorality is against society. But sin is against God."[8] Joseph resisted the temptation of Potiphar's wife by saying, "How then could I do such a wicked thing and sin *against God?*" (Genesis 39:9, italics added for emphasis) Similarly David wrote, referring to God, "*Against you*, you only, have I sinned and done what is evil in your sight, so that you are proved right when you speak and justified when you judge" (Psalm 51:4, italics added for emphasis). Clearly David's sin with Bathsheba had far-reaching effects on many relationships, but it began with a sin against God.

The Old Testament prophet Hosea painted a portrait of sin as *breaking covenant with God.*

Where does sin begin? Commentators from Augustine to C. S. Lewis have identified pride as the source of our sinfulness.[9] Too, sin often starts with unbelief. We hear it in the tempter's subtle dismissal of God's command, "Did God really say. . .?" (Gen. 3:1). Later Paul wrote that his own people, the Jews, were estranged from God because of their own unbelief (Romans 11:20). The Book of Hebrews confirms that some were not able to enter relationship with God because they refused to believe (Hebrews 3:19).

In the New Testament, Paul described sin as *idolatry* (Rom. 1:22–25). Idolatry is deeply rooted in pride. Humankind claimed wisdom, while foolishly exchanging the glory of the immortal God for images made to look like mortal human beings (Rom. 1:25).[10]

Are there degrees of sin? Some have distinguished between *mortal* and *venial* sins.[11] Are all sins equal in the eyes of God? Facing the casuistry of the Pharisees head on, Jesus answered them and defined sin more carefully in the Sermon on the Mount with a series of antitheses, "You have heard that it was said to the people long ago. . . . But I tell you. . ." (Matthew 5:21–42). Effectively Jesus moved sin from the action to the motive beneath it, confronting anyone who had avoided the action of murder but engaged in the sin of uncontrolled anger. Of course murder hurts a victim worse than just getting angry at him. Still, the attitude itself is tantamount to sin. The Book of James further reminds us, "For whoever keeps the whole law and yet stumbles at just one point is guilty of breaking all of it" (James 2:10).

What if we meant no harm by our actions? Sin need not be a matter of choice to offend a holy God. David wrote, "Who can discern his errors? Forgive my hidden faults" (Ps. 19:12).

When I was growing up in Germany, my best friend and I went with his family on a retreat along the Rhein River. Like Tom Sawyer and Huck Finn, the two of us took a raft out into a small harbor off the river. The current flowed out toward the middle of the river, and so periodically we needed to row back into the harbor. Eventually, drifting on the warm summer day, we both dozed off, only to awaken to the loud blare of a fog horn. We found ourselves in the center of the river with a barge bearing down on us. Quickly we rowed in full reverse to safety. We did not intend to endanger ourselves, but our slothful inactivity led us to great danger. Often without rebellious design we unintentionally drift into sin and miss the mark God has purposed for us.

On other occasions, we sin willfully. David sought to avoid this rebellion with the continuation of his prayer, "Keep your servant also from willful sins; may they not rule over me. Then will I be blameless, innocent of great transgression" (Ps.19:13). When tempted, we can pray for God to keep us from rebellion against him. With David, we pray, "May the words of my mouth and the meditation of my heart be pleasing in your sight, O LORD, my Rock and my Redeemer" (Ps. 19:14).

Whom does sin affect? Ultimately, sin affects all of humankind. Paul wrote to the church in Rome, "All have sinned and fall short of the glory of God" (Rom. 3:23). Sin creates havoc in human lives. The ultimate result is death. God told Adam and Eve that they would die if they ate from the tree of knowledge of good and evil (Gen. 2:17).

Who is responsible for sin? During the time of the Exile, the Old Testament prophet Ezekiel clarified our individual responsibility for our behavior, "The soul who sins is the one who will die" (Ezekiel 18:20). "The wages of sin is death," Paul concluded (Rom. 6:23).

Our Heritage: A Long Line of Sinners

When did sin begin? Genesis 1:31 tells us that on the sixth day of creation, God made humankind in his image and called the whole creation "very good." But by the end of Genesis 3, something had gone awry, and the very fabric of creation was torn as relationship with God was disrupted. To understand the story of salvation, we must understand the story of sin. In the Garden of Eden, the serpent tempted Eve and Adam to sin, and they succumbed.

Some years ago, *Newsweek* magazine reported about Kirsten Coulson, a Londoner who said she would be getting a plastic Christmas tree the next year. Given her experience, we might have made the same decision. The real tree she had purchased came with a surprise. When she was setting it up in her home, a real snake lurking in the real branches came out and bit her.[12]

Adam and Eve had a similar experience in the Garden of Eden. This crafty creature subtly seduced them, and they succumbed to sin (Gen. 3:6).

What do Adam and Eve's choices have to do with us? Paul wrote, "Therefore just as sin entered the world through one man, and death through sin, and in this way death came to all men, because all sinned" (Rom. 5:12). How did Adam and Eve's choice affect humankind as a whole? Unfortunately sin did not stop with Adam and Eve. Their son Cain killed their son Abel in anger. Did Adam's sin predispose humankind to sin by some genetic transmission of *original sin,* or was he representative of the weakness of all of humankind?[13]

We have all sinned, but why have we sinned? Is it Adam's fault or our own? Even if we dismiss the idea that sin is transmitted biologically, we remain part of a fallen human race going back to the sins of our earliest ancestors.[14] The human will has been compromised, making it difficult to resist sin. Does sin begin with our heredity, with our choices, or with supernatural forces at work in the world?[15]

Our Personal History: I Made Myself Do It

The story of Adam and Eve's fall feels eerily familiar because we all face the subtle presence of the tempter. Paul reminds us that Satan can disguise himself as an angel of light (2 Corinthians 11:14). Questioning the goodness of God, the tempter still asks today, "Did God really say. . . ?" (Gen. 3:1). Sin tempts us to disbelieve and doubt God.

Sin is "unbelieving disobedience."[16] Like Adam and Eve we may focus on the things God disallows instead of seeing the much larger range of good opportunities God makes available to us. Remember that in the Genesis story, our life-affirming Creator said *yes* to all of Eden except the tree of knowledge of good and evil (Gen. 2:15–17). Questioning the truthfulness of God, the serpent asserted, "You will not surely die" (Gen. 3:4).

Like Adam and Eve, the more we look, the more we like sin. When Eve saw that the fruit was good for food and pleasing to the eye and also desirable for gaining wisdom, she took some and ate it (Gen. 3:6). Pastor, professor, and author Eugene Peterson points out, "Every temptation that comes to me is packaged as a good."[17] For Adam and Eve, not only did it *look* good, but it *sounded* good to know as God knows. In the final analysis, for our ancestors and for us, nothing in the whole created world is as good as relationship with God, the Creator.

In truth, temptation is not the real reason for our sin. We can question about our own lives something our ancestors Adam and Eve did. That is, why were Adam and Eve hanging around the forbidden tree? We endanger our relationship with God when we become too familiar with sin and thus become acclimated and finally desensitized to it. To get in trouble in a place, we must first go there. So often, we loiter around the very temptations we know to be dangerous to our souls. What *trees* allure us? We need to identify the places, people, and situations that lead to bad decisions. We can choose to stay out of those places and situations and avoid the negative influence of those people.

Do we see the grace in God's pursuit of Adam and Eve? While they hid from God, God came walking, pursuing fellowship with them, asking, "Where are you?" (Gen. 3:9) In Frances Thompson's poem, "The Hound of Heaven," we hear the truth about our loving heavenly Father, who pursues us even when we flee from him.

> I fled Him, down the nights and down the days;
> I fled Him, down the arches of the years;
> I fled Him, down the labyrinthine ways
> Of my own mind; and in the mist of tears
> I hid from Him. . . .[18]

Adam did not answer God's question about where he was. Still evasive, he acknowledged that something had changed. God's questions still echo in the hearts of all who have chosen to disobey by omission or commission: "Who told you that you were naked? Have you eaten from the tree that I commanded you not to eat from?" (Gen. 3:11).

In the story of the first sin, each character in turn tried to blame somebody else. Adam tried to blame the woman and ultimately God when he said, "The woman you put here with me—she gave me some fruit from the tree, and I ate it" (Gen. 3:12). God turned to Eve to confront her choice, "What is this you have done?" Eve tried to blame the serpent, "The serpent deceived me, and I ate" (Gen. 3:13) Even so, God held them responsible.[19]

The New Testament Book of James makes clear that we cannot blame God for our choices. "When tempted, no one should say, 'God is tempting me.' For God cannot be tempted by evil, nor does he tempt anyone" (James 1:13). We can't blame others either, as tempting as that may be. One wonders if the Humpty Dumpty rhyme were being written today, the conclusion might be that Humpty Dumpty was pushed.[20] In our world, evasion of responsibility has become an art form.

We all bear responsibility for our own actions.[21] Some have suggested we need a *Statue of Responsibility* on the West coast of the United States to balance the Statue of Liberty on the East coast. Certainly liberty without responsibility wreaks havoc. In his writings, Paul helps us to accept responsibility, "So then, I myself in my mind am a slave to God's law, but in the sinful nature a slave to the law of sin" (Rom. 7:25). On another occasion, he admitted he was the "the worst" of sinners (1 Timothy 1:15). Even more pointedly, John confronts every evasion of responsibility, "If we claim we have not sinned, we make [God] out to be a liar and his word has no place in our lives" (1 John 1:10).

Our Broken World: Continuing Cosmic Consequences of Sin

How does God respond to our sin? In Romans, the Apostle Paul clarified the consequences of our sin: "The wrath of God is being revealed against all the godlessness and wickedness of men who suppress the truth by their wickedness" (Rom. 1:18–32).

The idea of wrath may make us uncomfortable. Consider this, though. Pastor and author Tim Keller writes, "Anger is not the opposite of love. Hatred is the opposite of love."[22] In other words, one can be both loving and angry. If you really love someone, you can be angry about their hurting and pain. Naturally, we become angry about that because we want something different for them.

Just so, God wants much more for us than sin offers, more than our disobedience would ever allow us to experience. Truly, God is angry at sin. Undeniably, God loves us. Certainly, God stopped at nothing to reach us. To our astonishment, God allowed his only Son to die rather than allow us to spend eternity without him.

Do you find it easier to see the sins of others than your own? I do. Even so, what is called *general revelation* leaves all sinners without excuse. That is, God reveals his power and his presence in the world so that all we need to know about God can be seen in nature. Accordingly, no one can excuse sin by saying, *Well, I just didn't know there was a God.* No one can truthfully plead ignorance, because God has manifested his presence. I saw it recently after a gloomy, cloudy, wintry kind of morning that mirrored our emotions as we gathered for a funeral service. Afterward, I went up to my study. Later that afternoon I emerged from my cocoon and looked outside. The sky was azure blue, filled with radiant, resplendent light, and I remembered Psalm 19:1 "The heavens declare the glory of God." I looked and listened as the skies shouted God's glory to everyone who had ears to hear.

Not only did Paul say we can see God in the world but also that God can see us in the world. God sees in our sinful choices the abysmal exchanges humankind has made. Guilty of idolatry, people exchanged God's glory for images made by humanity. In many businesses in the city in which I live, proprietors display statues of Buddha and other idols. Although we may never bow down to a statue of a god, we too are guilty. Idolatry is more common than we think in our postmodern world. The real American idol is not a singer on the popular television show. Like the ancient Romans, we worship the created things instead of the Creator so easily. As John Calvin said, "Our hearts are idol making factories."[23]

Next in Romans 1, Paul identified the exchange of God's design for homosexuality (Rom. 1:24–27). There are many discussions about how the church can best minister to homosexuals. We must be clear that God's standards have not changed. Any behavior that ever was wrong still is.[24] In the next passage, Paul confronted many other sins (Rom. 1:28–31). He wrote,

> They have become filled with every kind of wickedness, evil, greed and depravity. They are full of envy, murder, strife, deceit and malice. They are gossips, slanderers, God-haters, insolent, arrogant and boastful; they invent ways of doing evil; they disobey their parents; they are sense-less, faithless, heartless, ruthless (Rom 1:29–31).

At this point, if Paul were preaching in our churches, he might have heard a hearty *amen!* Uncomfortably for us, Paul wrote next, "You, therefore, have no excuse" (Rom. 2:1). In other words, sin was not just *their* problem; it is also *our* problem. Paul continued, "At whatever point you judge the other, you are condemning yourself, because you who pass judgment do the same things" (Rom. 2:3). Russian author Alexander Solzhenitsyn (1918–2008) wrote,

> If only there were evil people somewhere, insidiously committing evil deeds, and it were necessary only to separate them from the rest of us and destroy them. But the line dividing good and evil cuts through the heart of every human being. And who is willing to destroy a piece of his own heart?[25]

Evil is not consigned to a place *over there* somewhere, but the line of evil run through *our own hearts*.

Is God being unloving to warn that sin will lead us to destruction? To the contrary, God demonstrates great love and kindness. In loving judgment, God not only reveals our sin to us but also releases us to our sin. We find three times in Romans 1 the words God "gave them over" (Rom. 1:24, 26, 28). He allowed sinners to go where they wanted to go.[26] The Apostle Paul argued that these sins were manifestations of the wrath of God, punishments inflicted on rebellious humanity.

Why? Perhaps God gives us over to sin because God knows that when we continue down that path, we may come to a point where we recognize that God's very kindness and love will lead us to repentance (Rom. 2:4). Will we allow God's love to lead us back to him?

God gives humankind over to sin, not because God wants us to continue, but because at the end of the day, hell is the ultimate monument to human freedom. Hell is God letting people go their own way.

We cannot include Christ *in* our lives without subtracting sin *from* our lives. Indeed, when the Spirit of Holiness comes to live within believers, the Spirit starts doing enormous, amazing, wide-scale house cleaning. Thus, God's Spirit begins to eliminate and eradicate all sin from our lives. Failing to grow progressively in love of God and holiness and in our hatred for sin may well indicate we have no relationship with the Savior.

Results of Sin

We return to Adam and Eve to discover the results of their sin. As we have seen, when God came and asked whether they had eaten the forbidden fruit, Adam blamed God and his wife, "The woman you put here with me—she gave me some fruit from the tree, and I ate it" (Gen. 3:12). God then confronted Eve, and she answered, "The serpent deceived me, and I ate" (Gen. 3:13). Even though they blamed others, ultimately they had to accept the fact that they had chosen to sin.

Sooner or later, we all sit down to a big banquet of *consequences*. After Adam and Eve chose to sin, God confronted their choice and punished them. What are the consequences of sin?

First, for the first time humankind experienced shame (Gen. 3:10–11). Previously, Adam and Eve had felt no shame. After they sinned, they covered themselves (Gen. 2:25; 3:7). Mark Twain suggested that humans are the only creatures who blush and the only ones who need to.[27] To this day, guilt paralyzes those who have sinned. It comes as a result of the condemnation we feel in the presence of a holy God (John 3:18).

Further, humankind experienced suffering and the disruption of God's design and purpose (Gen. 3:14–19). God consigned the serpent to crawl through the dust (causing us to wonder how it traveled before). As a result of sin, Eve and her female descendants would experience pain in childbirth. Instead of receiving food from the garden, Adam would have to work by the sweat of his brow.

Sin still creates untold suffering in the lives of those who succumb to it. This is not to say that all suffering in our lives is a direct and immediate judgment from God on some specific sin. Our sinful world is a fallen world where we experience the consequences of sin as a part of the judgment on all creation. Paul expressed this consequence in a great crescendo,

> I consider that our present sufferings are not worth comparing with the glory that will be revealed in us. The creation waits in eager expectation for the sons of God to be revealed. For the creation was subjected to frustration, not by its own choice but by the will of the one who subjected it, in hope that the creation itself will be liberated from its bondage to decay and brought into the glorious freedom of the children of God (Rom. 8:18–21).

As a cosmic power, sin entraps and enslaves.[28] "Don't you know that when you offer yourselves to someone to obey him as slaves, you are slaves to the one whom you obey—whether you are slaves to sin, which leads to death, or to obedience, which leads to righteousness?" (Rom. 6:16). A few verses later, Paul continued, "We know that the law is spiritual, but I am unspiritual, sold as a slave to sin" (Rom. 7:14). Sinners may want to do well but find themselves unable to do so. Philosophy professor, speaker, and author Dallas Willard, a Baptist, has it right, "We want to do well, but we are prepared to do evil."[29]

This enslavement to sin becomes the source of our depravity, which can be defined as "our human inability or powerlessness to remedy our dire situation."[30] To say we are depraved is not to say we are always as bad as we could be but that at no point are we as good as we should be.

Sin ultimately involves the whole person.[31] No part of our person is unaffected by sin.[32] Even more, *depravity* means we are totally incapable of solving our own sin problem or extricating ourselves from the bondage it brings.[33]

Sin kills. To sin is to die. We hear it in God's initial warning, "when you eat of it you will surely die" (Gen. 2:17). To this day, "the wages of sin is death" (Rom. 6:23). The consequence of sin is not just that we die someday. We could place that idea—someday—out of our minds. Instead, death, like a job, pays us day by day. Paul did not call sin a sickness but death when he wrote, "You were dead in your transgressions and sins" (Ephesians 2:1). Spiritual death results in eternal separation from God (Revelation 21:8).[34]

This separation or isolation from God remains sin's worst consequence. Sin alienates humankind from God.[35] Evicted from the Garden, Adam and Eve lost not only God's beautiful provision and purpose but also immediate access to close fellowship with God. They had walked and talked with God, but they lost the intimacy they had enjoyed with God. The ensuing story recorded in Genesis 4—11 deteriorates to fratricide, a flood, and the dispersion of humankind across the earth through the confusion of languages.

Genesis 1—11 paints a picture of the problem of humankind. The remainder of the Scriptures tells the story of God's solution, culminating in God sending his only Son into the world to save people from their sin. Truly, "the wages of sin is death, but the gift of God is eternal life in Christ Jesus our Lord" (Rom. 6:23).

The recent movie *Amazing Grace* offers an historical account of the work of William Wilberforce (1759-1833) and John Newton (1725-1807). Wilberforce fought the sin of slavery as a member of Parliament in England. John Newton, his pastor, wrote the song "Amazing Grace." Early in the story Wilberforce went to Newton and said, "I know you used to be a slave trader. If you could write down all the names of the ships and the ports, then I could use that to overturn the slave trade in England." The abolition of the slave trade was Wilberforce's great passion. Newton answered in agony, "I can't do that. I can't remember all those things because that brings back

20,000 ghosts of people who died on my ships, and I don't want to think about that any more."

Later in the movie, however, Newton contacted Wilberforce again. By this time, Newton had lost his sight. Having remembered and recorded his experiences, he said, "Here it is. Here are the accounts. Here are the names and the ports and the ships—all of my memories. Use these notes to overturn slavery in our country." Then he said, "I forget many things these days, but I remember two things: I am a great sinner and Christ is a great Savior."

Newton's story is also ours. We are great sinners. We can be thankful that Christ is a great Savior.

CHAPTER *Three*

God's Provision of Salvation

Salvation Is Here

> "For the Son of Man came to seek
> and to save what was lost."
>
> —LUKE **19:10**

HAVE YOU EVER LOST ANYTHING of great value? Did you find it? How did you feel? Imagine Bill Fulton's joy when somebody found his wallet recently. In Baker City, Oregon, he opened his door only to discover that his long-lost wallet had been discovered. Fulton lost it sixty-three years earlier in the Baker Middle School gym while cheering for his team. The school secretary brought it to Fulton. He had ceased looking for the wallet long ago, but a man who was renovating the gym found it.[1]

This is our story, too. We once were lost, but now we have been found. Even though we may feel forgotten, the heavenly Father sent his only Son to seek us and to save us. When nobody else was even looking, God found a way to find us and bring us home to himself.

How does the Bible describe salvation? As we saw in chapter one, the Old Testament uses many different words for salvation, and each captures part of the meaning. The first and most frequent word, *haya*, simply means *to give life*. Another word, *yasha*, means *to bring out into a spacious environment*. Still another word, *go'el*, speaks of the kinsman-redeemer who purchased his deceased kinsman's land and married his wife in order to save his relative's heritage. A fourth word, *padah*, means *ransom* or *substitution*. [2]

In the New Testament, we find the word *soteria*, which means *wholeness* or *wellness*. Other words provide the image that we have been redeemed and delivered. Ultimately, salvation is the gift of life.[3] Further, salvation is inextricably intertwined with Jesus. Peter preached to the very ones who had crucified Jesus in Jerusalem, "Salvation is found in no one else" (Acts 4:12). All of heaven sings, "Salvation belongs to our God, who sits on the throne, and to the Lamb" (Revelation 7:10). The One who owns salvation is the King.

Election: The King Chooses to Love

The idea of election or God choosing his people finds deep roots in the Old Testament. In the prophecy of Malachi we read, "'I have loved you,' says the LORD. 'But you ask, "How have you loved us?" 'Was not Esau Jacob's brother?' the LORD says, 'Yet I have loved Jacob, but Esau I have hated'" (Malachi 1:2–3). Election reminds us that salvation begins in the heart of God himself. Our loving God pursues a plan to save people.[4]

Jesus illuminates election with these words to his disciples, "You did not choose me, but I chose you and appointed you to go and bear fruit—fruit that will last" (John 15:16). In this case, Jesus had literally chosen his disciples. This choice did not void or hinder their free will, however. When John the Baptist said to his disciples, "Look, the Lamb of God," they decided to follow Jesus and obey his summons, "Come, and you will see" (John 1:35, 39).

How can we hold together the seemingly contradictory ideas that a sovereign God chooses to save while humans continue to exercise free will? Can God know the future and simultaneously allow us to make free choices? W. T. Conner, a highly respected Baptist theologian of an earlier generation, answered those who doubted God's foreknowledge, ". . . The position that foreknowledge on God's part excludes freedom on man's part is wholly gratuitous."[5] For example, at Pentecost, Peter said to those who crucified Jesus that the Lord had been "handed over to you *by God's set purpose and foreknowledge*; and *you*, with the help of wicked men, *put him to death* by nailing him to the cross" (Acts 2:23, italics added for emphasis). Similarly, when caught in a storm on the way to Rome, Paul asserted on the one hand that God had told him he and all on the ship with him would be spared, but on the other hand that if the sailors tried to escape in the lifeboats they would all die (Acts 27:22, 31). The Scriptures hold the ideas of God's sovereignty and free will in tension, and so must we. Conner asks, "How can a thing be fixed or certain in God's mind and contingent so far as man is concerned? No man can tell. But that does not mean that it cannot be."[6]

Are some predestined to be saved and others predestined to be lost? Christians have debated this idea through the ages. Some have gone beyond the scriptural teaching on election, while others have omitted reference to it altogether. Interestingly, the Scriptures nowhere place the concept of election in the position of philosophical debate or speculation but in the context of gratitude and praise. On the heels of Paul's great crescendo, "And we know that in all things God works for the good of those who love him, who have been called according to his purpose," Paul continued, "For those God foreknew he also predestined to be conformed to the likeness of his Son, that he might be the firstborn among many brothers. And those he predestined he also called; those he called, he also justified; those he justified, he also glorified" (Romans 8:28–29). These verses do not answer the question of who will be saved but rather remind us that God's purpose will be fulfilled.[7]

Using the analogy of Jacob and Esau, Paul argued for the justice of God, writing, "Yet, before the twins were born or had done anything good or bad—in order that God's purpose in election might stand: not by works but by him who calls—she was told, 'The older will serve the younger'" (Rom. 9:11-12). He spelled out the point of election, "It does not therefore depend on man's desire or effort, but on God's mercy" (Rom. 9:16).

Similarly, in his letter to the Christians at Ephesus, Paul emphasized that the God and Father of our Lord Jesus Christ "chose us in him before the creation of the world to be holy and blameless in his sight. In love he predestined us to be adopted as his sons through Jesus Christ, in accordance with his pleasure and will—to the praise of his glorious grace which he has freely given us in the One he loves" (Ephesians 1:4-6). Corresponding with his discussion of the Father, the Son, and the Holy Spirit, Paul culminated with a paeon of praise— "to the praise of his glorious grace," "for the praise of his glory," and "to the praise of his glory" (Eph. 1:6, 12, 14).

Especially in the same letter, we notice Paul's emphasis on election as a corporate experience. "In [Christ] *we* were also chosen" (Eph. 1:11, italics added for emphasis). We are elected "to" community and "for" community.[8] God chose Abraham to be father of a people who would not only be blessed but be a blessing (Genesis 12:3). He further chose his people Israel to be a missionary people to reach both the Israelites and the surrounding nations (Isaiah 42:1; 49:6). God has chosen us in Christ to be his people on mission in the world today.

Historically, Augustine (354-430) and Calvin (1509-1564) interpreted Romans 9–11 as emphasizing the idea that "God has total control over human beings and chooses some for salvation but passes over others."[9] They also presumed that Christ died for the elect alone. Inevitably, God brings the elect to faith and repentance so they are justified and preserves them in faith so they do not fall away. The Dutch theologian Jacob Arminius (1560-1609), on the other hand, held that God's election of human beings to salvation was dependent on God's foreknowledge of what they would freely do.[10]

Does God choose some to be saved and others to be lost? New Testament professor I. Howard Marshall shows us how Paul answered these questions. First, Paul assumed that the death of Christ includes all people (Rom. 5:18, 11:32). Second, Paul did not argue that God arbitrarily dispenses mercy but that we can not compel him to be merciful to us (Rom. 9:15). Third, Paul's language of predestination refers to what God purposes to do with people who have come to faith and to God's purpose in creating a people, not to his purpose to save some individuals and not others.(Rom. 8:33; 11:7; Colossians 3:12). Paul never applied the term *elect* to potential believers but to those who had already come to faith. Fourth, by praying for Israel to behave differently, Paul assumed they had the real potential to do so (Rom. 10:1). Fifth, God is still appealing to Israel by making them envious of the Gentiles (Rom. 11:14).[11] Paul holds in tension the idea of God's sovereignty and the concept that people are saved or lost depending on whether they believe. We are called to live in this tension.

Unquestionably, God alone initiates salvation. Our decision to follow Christ confirms our election. The New Testament teaches that we must believe in order to be God's children. How do we respond to God's electing love? We live "to the praise of his glorious grace" (Eph. 1:6). The nineteenth-century evangelist D. L. Moody is reported to have said, "The elect are the *whosoever wills* and the non-elect are the *whosoever won'ts.*"

Incarnation: The King Has Arrived

What were the people of Jesus' day looking for? Bible scholar N. T. Wright states that the people of that time were actually waiting for God to come and deliver them from exile.[12] Ever since the Exile recorded in the Old Testament, including the time when the people returned to Israel beginning in 538 B.C., the people of God were looking for God to come and save them. For many, this expectation took the form of a political hope. Who would deliver Israel from Rome, their latest conqueror?

A baby born in Bethlehem must have seemed an unlikely candidate. We hear in Jesus' name (derived from the Hebrew *yasha*) that his mission was not only to seek but also to save. Early in Matthew's account of the nativity, an angel promised Joseph that Mary would give birth to a son. The angel commanded that the child be given "the name Jesus, because he will save his people from their sins" (Matthew 1:21). Matthew shows us again and again that the coming of Christ fulfilled the Old Testament prophecies (Matt. 1:22–23; 2:5–6, 15, 17, 23). "All this took place to fulfill what the Lord had said through the prophet: 'The virgin will be with child and will give birth to a son, and they will call him "Immanuel"—which means, 'God with us'" (Matt. 1:22–23). Some time later, the Magi or Wise Men, likely from the geographical area of present-day Iran, came asking for the king of the Jews. This confounded and angered the Idumaean usurper Herod.[13] The wise men were not really kings but astronomers or astrologers.[14] Herod, a descendant of Esau, was a mere pretender to power. But Israel's real King, Jesus, the true descendant of David, was born as King.

Every king rules over a kingdom. John the Baptist's and Jesus' first sermons mirrored each other, "Repent for the kingdom of heaven is near" (Matt. 3:2; 4:17). By calling for repentance, both Jesus and John the Baptist revealed that the new kingdom required a radical shift in direction for all who would be citizens. By *kingdom*, they were not talking about a geographical location but about the presence and reign of the King among them. People recognized Jesus' authority in his teaching (Matt. 7:28–29; John 7:45–46). When Jesus performed miracles, they knew he was a prophet, and they sought to make him their "king by force" (John 6:14–15).

In Jesus, heaven's King and kingdom came near. All heaven broke loose on earth when Jesus came. He fulfilled the Old Testament kingship of God.

When the people came to Samuel in a petition for a king that led to the anointing of Israel's first King Saul, God told Samuel, ". . . It is not you they have rejected, but they have rejected me. . ." (1 Samuel 8:6–7). For years after King Saul, Israel and Judah had lived under their own fallible kings and then under foreign kings. Now, Jesus their true King had returned. Jesus came to save from sins and also to rule as sovereign King over his followers as their Lord. The richness of Jesus' ministry, which is encapsulated in the phrase *kingdom of heaven* (or *kingdom of God*) implies so much more than the forgiveness of sin. It is, in fact, the rule or reign of Christ as Lord in the lives of his followers. The kingdom of heaven marks the arrival of heaven on earth.

A man known as Father Damien left Belgium and landed in Honolulu, Hawaii, in 1864. Before long he moved to the village of Kalawao on the Island of Molokai. There Father Damien ministered to the people who suffered from Hansen's disease. For sixteen years he shared his life with them, learning to speak their language, bandaging their wounds, embracing the bodies no one else would touch, and preaching to hearts that would otherwise have been left alone. While there, Father Damien organized schools, bands, and choirs. He built homes so the people could have shelter. In love, he built 2,000 coffins by hand so that, when people died, they could be buried with dignity. Slowly, it was said, Kalawao became a place to live rather than a place to die, for Father Damien offered hope. Immersed in the world of people suffering from Hansen's disease, Father Damien was not careful about keeping his distance. For Father Damien's nearness to them, the people loved him. One day, however, he noticed a numbness in his extremities. He found he himself had Hansen's disease, commonly referred to as leprosy. When he next stood to preach to the people, he began, "We lepers. . . ."[15] Now Father Damien was not only one who cared for the lepers. He was one of them.

Why did God send his Son? Why did Jesus come into the world? Love. "For God so loved the world that he gave his one and only Son. . ." (John 3:16). The story of incarnation begins in the heart of God. "In the beginning was the Word, and the Word was with God, and the Word was God" (John 1:1). This "Word" (Greek *logos*) represents the Son of God. The Gospel of John continues, "The Word became flesh and made his dwelling among us" (John 1:14). Paul captured the same thought in the beautiful hymn he recorded in his letter to Philippi, "Your attitude should be the same as that of Christ Jesus: Who being in very nature God, did not consider equality with God something to be grasped, but made himself nothing, taking the very nature of a servant, being made in human likeness" (Philippians 2:5–7).

As love caused the Father to send his only Son, it also compelled the Son to search for and save those who were lost. As Jesus described it on the day Zacchaeus was transformed in Jericho, "The Son of man came to seek and to save what was lost" (Luke 19:10).

Why did Jesus come? Jesus came to seek the lost. Have you ever been lost? Navigationally impaired, I have lost my way a number of times. When my older brothers and I were students at Baylor University in Waco, Texas, our parents lived in Montana. After we completed our final exams, we packed our car and headed out to make the thirty-hour drive home without stopping to sleep. This schedule usually put us into Amarillo, Texas, late in the evening. Often my brothers and I would exchange places as drivers, and then the ones who were not driving went to sleep. From Dalhart, Texas, we were supposed to go over into New Mexico and then up toward Colorado and Wyoming. More than once, one of the brothers would awaken the other two of us and ask, "What are we doing in Oklahoma?" We were lost again!

Jesus told three stories about things lost and found. Luke recounted these three parables in response to Jesus' encounter with those who looked askance at all the "sinners" gathered around Jesus (Luke 15). It bothered the religious aristocracy that Jesus ate with "sinners." Jesus used the term "lost" in the three consecutive stories to show the Father's heart for those who had lost their way.

First, Jesus spoke of a solitary sheep that wandered from its flock of 100 (Luke 15:1–7). The loving shepherd left the ninety-nine in the open country to go after the one lost sheep. Similarly, a woman lost one of her ten coins (Luke 15:8–10). She lit a lamp, swept the house, and searched carefully. She did not stop searching until she found the coin. The final and most familiar of the three stories introduces to us a father who had two sons, one obedient and the other prodigal (Luke 15:11–32). *I wish you were dead*, the younger son implied, asking for his inheritance in advance. The father granted his wish, gave his inheritance, and allowed him to go. After the young man wasted the money on wild living and began to experience the consequences of his choices, he came to himself and returned to his father. His father saw him when he was a long way off. It seems that the whole time since his son had left, the father had been waiting and watching for him to come home. This portrait shows us what Jesus means when he says he comes to seek and to save the lost. As in the story, Jesus not only wants to find us, but he also wants to save us from the wandering of a sheep, the useless-ness of an unspent coin, and the wasted life of a prodigal child.

The incarnation of Christ marks God's most direct intervention on earth for the salvation of humankind, but it does not complete the story. The crucifixion brings atonement or restoration of our rela-tionship with God.[16] How did Jesus save the lost? In his own words, "The Son of Man did not come to be served, but to serve, and to give his life as a ransom for many" (Matt. 20:28).

Crucifixion: The King Is Sacrificed

Touring the Holy Land enables one to see many impressive sights. None perhaps is more gripping than the stone face of the skull-like rock formation at Gordon's Calvary. There is some debate about whether Gordon's Calvary is the actual site of Christ's cross, but there is no doubt that it looks like the description of the place of the crucifixion.[17]

On our tour, devoted and erudite students of the Scriptures served as tour guides. One of our groups followed a wonderful British gentle-man up the hill thought to be Golgotha. A woman from another tour group asked him as they surveyed the hillside, "Where exactly was Jesus crucified?" The wise gentleman responded reverently, "Ma'am, I cannot tell you *where* Jesus was crucified, but I can tell you *why* he was crucified. It was for our sins."[18]

God answered the sin of humankind by sending his only Son Jesus Christ into the world. Jesus the Savior gives the gift of salvation to all who will receive it (John 1:12-13). Let's think together about God our King's marvelous provision of salvation.

Jesus taught about the kingdom of heaven or, as Mark and Luke call it, the kingdom of God. The theme of Christ as King reemerges at the end of the Gospels (Matt. 27:27-29; Mark 15:32; Luke 23:37-38; John 18:33-37; 19:1-5) when those who crucified Jesus referred to him as "the King of the Jews." Jesus' purple robe and crown of thorns emphasized the suffering of the King. Although the insig-nia over the cross intended to mock Jesus, instead it confirmed the truth. He was the King. By his death King Jesus procured salvation for others.

The Apostle Paul wrote of this theme in his letters to the churches. Most notably, we hear it echoed in his letter to the Colossians, "Giving thanks to the Father, who has qualified you to share in the inheritance of the saints in the kingdom of light. For he has rescued us from the dominion of darkness and brought us into the kingdom of the Son he loves, in whom we have redemption, the forgiveness of sins" (Colossians 1:12).

Paul distinguished God's kingdom from "the dominion of darkness" and called it "the kingdom of light." The King is the Son whom the Father loves, Jesus. Further, God's kingdom is about love, redemption, and forgiveness. Finally, this kingdom offers a rich inheritance for its citizens who are known as saints. The Bible does not use the words "saints" as a subset of super-Christians. Saints are literally all believers who have been made holy by Christ.

The Cross as Victory: Victory over the Dominion of Darkness

We often see news stories of dramatic deliverance from the forces of nature or hostile military actions. Colossians 1:13 states that Jesus "has rescued us." What did Jesus do? First, he "rescued us from the dominion of darkness" (Col. 1:13). In the Gospels, we observe Jesus facing and defeating Satan in the wilderness temptations (Matt. 4:1–11, Mark 1:12–13, Luke 4:1–13). Jesus "was led by the Spirit into the desert to be tempted by the devil" (Matt. 4:1). There the tempter came to him, seeking to entice Jesus to transform stones into bread, leap from the temple precipice, and bow down and worship him. In each instance, Jesus answered the devil with words of Scripture (Matt. 4:2–13). Frequently Jesus delivered people from demonic possession (Matt. 8:28–34). In every instance, our Lord demonstrated the supremacy of his authority over the forces of evil in our world. On the cross Jesus consummated his great victory over the forces of Satan, sin, and death.

In Ephesians, Paul painted an even more detailed picture of this hierarchy of evil spiritual forces in the world: "Finally, be strong in the Lord and in his mighty power. Put on the full armor of God so that you can take your stand against the devil's schemes. For our struggle is not against flesh and blood, but against the rulers, against the authorities, against the powers of this dark world and against spiritual forces of evil in the heavenly realms" (Eph. 6:10–12). Satan is the embodiment of evil schemes against God's people. Paul reminded believers that we struggle against the devil, who is not a flesh-and-blood human being.

The devil is not alone. He presides over rulers and authorities and powers consisting of spiritual forces of evil. Their authority, although exercised on earth, resides primarily in the heavenly realms. Peter warned, "Your enemy the devil prowls around like a roaring lion looking for someone to devour" (1 Peter 5:8). Two risks present themselves to us here: first, to say less than the Scripture says about the power of Satan in the world; and second, to go beyond what the Scripture says and develop an elaborate understanding of evil not presented in the text.

Jesus has rescued us from the evil control of Satan. Again in his Letter to the Colossians, Paul said, "And having disarmed the powers and authorities, he made a public spectacle of them, triumphing over them by the cross" (Col. 2:15). On the cross, Jesus defeated the dominion of darkness. This view shows us "sin and salvation as a conflict between God and the devil."[19] God's holiness or righteousness always conflicts with sin. As long as the conflict was between humanity and sin, sin won. But on the cross God did battle with sin. So when Jesus died, he was not "the victim, but the victor."[20] Thus he overcame the "prince of this world" and drove him out (John 12:31).

On the cross, Jesus further won the victory over the law (Galatians 3:13) and over death with its connection to sin (Rom. 8:2). Some have used the analogy of D-Day in World War II to illustrate this victory. The D-Day invasion meant victory, even though the complete victory was not realized until months afterward. Perhaps a better analogy is declaring the end of World War II to the last Japanese soldier hiding in the Philippine jungle. Lieutenant Hiroo Onoda refused to believe that World War II was over, and remained in hiding from 1945 until

1974, when he was finally reached by a man named Norio Suzuki. Onoda had lived under a false view of the world, pledging allegiance to a long-defeated power, for twenty-nine years. Suzuki proclaimed to him the good news that the war was over, and Onoda finally brought his life and his behavior in line with the truth.[21] The proclamation of the truth that the war is over, the enemy is defeated, and all people can now live in the good news of the victory of Jesus is what evangelism is all about.

How do the forces of evil in the world threaten believers today? Temptation needs no introduction, for we are all tempted. Paul offers encouraging words: "No temptation has seized you except what is common to man. And God is faithful; he will not let you be tempted beyond what you can bear. But when you are tempted he will also provide a way out so that you can stand up under it" (1 Corinthians 10:13). The Book of Hebrews reminds us,

> For we do not have a high priest who is unable to sympathize with our weaknesses, but we have one who has been tempted in every way just as we are yet was without sin. Let us then approach the throne of grace with confidence, so that we may receive mercy and find grace to help us in our time of need (Hebrews 4:15).

Christ's victory becomes our victory. "Resist the devil, and he will flee from you" (James 4:7). As believers who have received salvation, we appropriate Christ's victory over evil by trusting our Savior, praying, actively resisting evil, and choosing obedience.

The Cross as Sacrificial Substitution

Perhaps the best-known theory of our atonement with God is known as *substitutionary atonement*. These words center on the truth that Christ took our place by dying on the cross. He satisfied the wrath of God by substituting himself for our sins. "Without the shedding of blood, there is no forgiveness" (Heb. 9:22). If the wages of sin is death, then someone must die because of sin. Instead of allowing us to die,

God sent his only Son to die in our place. Jesus Christ became our substitute.

Old Testament law required sacrifice, "For the life of the creature is in the blood, and I have given it to you to make atonement for yourselves on the altar; it is the blood that makes atonement for yourselves on the altar for one's life" (Leviticus 17:11). This passage teaches us three truths about the blood sacrifice. First, blood is the symbol of life. Second, blood makes atonement with God. Third, God who gives life gives the blood, so that the whole sacrificial system is God's idea.[22]

Sacrifice plays a prominent role in the Old Testament institution and celebration of the Passover (Exodus 12:2–17). In this light we understand the words of John the Baptist who introduced Jesus as the "Lamb of God, who takes away the sin of the world!" (John 1:29; see also 1:36). In Revelation as well, John referred to Jesus more than twenty-five times as the Lamb who was slain to purchase people for God (see, for example, Revelation 5:6, 8, 12, 13). No wonder Paul equated Christ's sacrifice with the fulfillment of the Passover, "Christ, our Passover lamb, has been sacrificed" (1 Corinthians 5:7–8). Jesus understood his ministry as the fulfillment of Isaiah's prophecy of the righteous Suffering Servant,[23]

> *Surely he took up our infirmities and carried our sorrows. . . . But he was pierced for our transgressions, he was crushed for our iniquities. . . . He was oppressed and afflicted, yet he did not open his mouth; he was led like a lamb to the slaughter and as a sheep before her shearers is silent, so he did not open his mouth (Isaiah 53:4, 5, 7).*

Paul summarized substitutionary sacrifice succinctly, "God made him who had no sin to be sin for us, so that in him we might become the righteousness of God" (2 Cor. 5:21). He further taught, "All have sinned and fall short of the glory of God" (Rom. 3:23). Because we have all sinned, we need a sinless substitute to become our Savior. The Book of Hebrews teaches that Jesus, our great High Priest, is able to sympathize with our weaknesses because he was "tempted in every way just as we are—yet was without sin" (Heb.4:15). We are sinners, and Jesus was sinless.

By Christ's death, he atoned for our sins. "He is the *atoning sacrifice* for our sins and not only for our sins but also for the sins of the whole world" (1 John 2:2, italics added for emphasis). God presented Jesus the Son as "a sacrifice of atonement" (Rom. 3:25). For this reason we do not speak of "God punishing Jesus or of Jesus persuading God, for to do so is to set them against each other as if they acted independently of each other or were even in conflict with each other."[24]

Theologian John Stott explains further, "The concept of substitution lies at the heart of both sin and salvation. For the essence of sin is man substituting himself for God, while the essence of salvation is God substituting himself for man."[25] Jesus was righteous, and we are unrighteous. By taking our sin on himself, Jesus made a way for us to become righteous, right with God, just as Jesus was right with God. Augustus Toplady captured it in the great hymn "Rock of Ages,"[26]

> In my hand no price I bring,
> Simply to Thy cross I cling.

The Cross as Ransom and Redemption

Bruce Prindle, a friend and fellow Texas pastor, served years ago as a summer missionary in Tennessee. Tragically, that summer a young man in the community was accidentally shot and killed. The boy's father, covered in his son's blood, came out of the emergency room after the young man passed away. Someone, in kindness, said, "Let's get you cleaned up." The desperately broken father said, "No. This blood is all that I have left of my son."

Imagine the love of our heavenly Father, his heart broken by the crucifixion of his Son, taking that very blood as the purchase price of the redemption of the world. No wonder Paul exclaimed to the church at Corinth, "You were bought at a price" (1 Cor. 6:20). We were, indeed.

Another way in which Bible scholars explain Christ's work on the cross is with the *ransom* theory of atonement. Jesus gave "his life as a ransom for many" (Mark 10:45). The biblical terms *ransom* and *redemption* describe the work of Christ without specifying to whom the ransom was paid.[27]

In the variegated tapestry of salvation portrayed in the New Testament, *redemption* offers one of the most beautiful portraits of all. *To redeem* is *to purchase* or *to buy back*. As we saw in chapter one, two stories from the Old Testament enrich our understanding of redemption.

The first emerges from the little Book of Ruth. When Naomi and her daughter-in-law Ruth returned to Israel from Moab as widows, they were destitute. As Ruth went to glean in the fields, by God's providence she worked in the field of a good man named Boaz. Boaz was related to her mother-in-law Naomi and so to Ruth's deceased husband. By Old Testament law, Boaz had the opportunity to purchase not only the land of Ruth's husband but also to marry her in the process, thus becoming her *go'el*, meaning *kinsman-redeemer*. In a beautiful love story, Boaz took Ruth as his wife. From their union came a child named Obed, who had a son named Jesse, who had a son named David, who became king of Israel. When David's descendant Jesus was born and purchased us with his own blood, Jesus became our *kinsman-redeemer* as well.

Another beautiful redemption story is that of Hosea and Gomer, found in the Book of Hosea. God told Hosea to marry "an adulterous wife" (Hosea 1:2).[28] Hosea did and discovered over time that she had become unfaithful to him. When she left him to pursue her sinful choices, he waited for her and raised the children. Finally, he went to her and purchased her at the price of a slave—"fifteen pieces of silver and a homer and lethech of barley" (Hosea 3:2). Having completed the transaction, he invited her to live with him faithfully (Hos. 3:3). He showed love to her—*chesed* or *covenant love*—in reuniting with her after she had left him. The story becomes a parable for Israel's unfaithfulness to God and God's redeeming love that would not let them go. Hosea's words find fulfillment in the story of Jesus, who gave his all to redeem us.

Especially in Jesus "we have redemption through his blood" (Eph. 1:7). With his blood, Jesus paid a price for us. Later, in a letter to his protégé Timothy, Paul wrote, "For there is one God and one mediator between God and men, the man Christ Jesus, who gave himself as a ransom for all men. . ." (1 Timothy 2:5–6). Jesus "gave himself for us to redeem us from all wickedness" (Titus 2:14). Peter echoed this theme, "For you know that it was not with perishable things such as silver or gold that you were redeemed from the empty way of life handed down to you from your forefathers, but with the precious blood of Christ, a lamb without blemish or defect" (1 Peter 1:18–19).

The Book of Hebrews elucidates the idea that Jesus, our high priest "entered the Most Holy Place once for all by his own blood, having obtained eternal redemption" (Heb. 9:12). Unlike the previous high priests who had "entered the Most Holy Place" by virtue of the blood of animals slain, Jesus came on the basis of his own "once for all" sacrifice. When we car-pooled to seminary, Wesley Shotwell, Alan LeFever, Paul Rummage, and I used to sing the great old hymn on the way from Waco to Fort Worth,

> Once for all, O sinner, receive it,
> Once for all, O brother, believe it;
> Cling to the cross, the burden will fall,
> Christ hath redeemed us once for all.[29]

Why did Jesus redeem us? In the final book of the New Testament we learn that the living creatures and elders fell down before the Lamb and sang a new song, "You are worthy to take the scroll and to open its seals, because you were slain, and with your blood you purchased men for God from every tribe and language and people and nation" (Rev. 5:9). Christ's death and shed blood purchased people. Christ purchased us for God because God wanted a people of his very own. As Scripture says, "God so loved the world. . ." (John 3:16).

The Cross as Example

These views of the atonement show that the primary purpose of the cross was not to offer us a *moral example,* as some scholars have taught.[30] As Bible scholar N.T. Wright has written, "Watching Tiger

Woods hit a golf ball doesn't inspire me to go out and copy him. It makes me realize that I can't come close and never will."[31]

Even so, again and again the New Testament writers call us to follow Christ's example. Jesus said, "If anyone would come after me, he must deny himself and take up his cross daily and follow me" (Luke 9:23). Paul urged the divided Philippians,

> *Your attitude should be the same as that of Christ Jesus: Who, being in very nature God, did not consider equality with God something to be grasped but made himself nothing, taking the very nature of a servant, being made in human likeness. And being found in appearance as a man, he humbled himself and became obedient to death—even death on a cross! (Philippians 2:5–8).*

The Apostle Peter found in the cross an example of patient suffering for Christians to emulate: "To this you were called, because Christ suffered for you, leaving you an example that you should follow in his steps" (1 Pet. 2:21). Thomas Shepherd wrote this hymn text,

> Must Jesus bear the cross alone,
> And all the world go free?
> No, there's a cross for everyone,
> And there's a cross for me.[32]

There is, after all, a great difference between simply admiring Jesus and actually following Jesus. We are to put the exemplary love of Christ into practice. "Be imitators of God, therefore, as dearly loved children and live a life of love, just as Christ loved us and gave himself up for us as a fragrant offering and sacrifice to God" (Eph. 5:1–2). In our relationships, we are to imitate the love, selflessness, and sacrifice of Christ. These actions do not supplement or complete our salvation, but they do show the world our connection with Christ.

As we consider the price Christ paid on the cross, we still hear the echo of his voice, *Follow after me.*[33] Luke 9:57–62 tells of Jesus' encounters with three would-be followers. One misunderstood where Jesus was going. Another wanted to bury his father first. The third desired to say good-by to his family. In each case Jesus insisted on the primacy of following him. Once we call Christ Lord we can never subsequently say as these did, *Let me first*. . . . The call of Christ is not just to *wear* a cross but to *bear* a cross. Salvation calls forth the learning and obedience of disciples who follow in Christ's steps.

Resurrection: The King Lives

The story of salvation includes but does not conclude with the cross. The New Testament points to the resurrection as the confirmation of Christ's great triumph. The risen Lord claimed "all authority in heaven and on earth" (Matt. 28:18). Peter preached at Pentecost, "Therefore let all Israel be assured of this: God has made this Jesus, whom you crucified, both Lord and Christ" (Acts 2:36). Confirming the resurrection and its importance, Paul wrote, "For [God] 'has put everything under his feet'" (1 Cor. 15:27). Notice the triumphant tone in Paul's letter to the church at Philippi, "Therefore God exalted him to the highest place and gave him the name that is above every name" (Phil. 2:9).

What difference does the resurrection make? The Corinthians were asking Paul that question (1 Cor. 15:12). Paul answered powerfully, "If Christ has not been raised. . ." (1 Cor. 15:14; see 15:12–19):

- · "There is no resurrection from the dead"
- · Our preaching is useless
- · Our "faith is futile"
- · We are "false witnesses about God"
- · We are "still in our sins"
- · Those who have passed away "are lost"
- · "We are to be pitied more than all men"

Paul confidently proclaimed, "But Christ has indeed been raised from the dead, the firstfruits of those who have fallen asleep" (1 Cor. 15:20). In a succinct description of the gospel, Paul urged the Romans, ". . . If you confess with your mouth, 'Jesus is Lord,' and believe in your heart that God raised him from the dead, you will be saved" (Rom.

10:9). Salvation remains impossible apart from faith in the risen Lord of life, Jesus Christ.

The poet and preacher John Donne (1572–1631) captured the triumphant implications of the resurrection,

> Death, be not proud, though some have called thee
> Mighty and dreadful, for thou art not so;
> For those, whom thou think'st, thou dost overthrow,
> Die not, poor Death, nor yet canst thou kill me.
>
> . . . .
>
> One short sleep past, we wake eternally,
> And Death shall be no more; Death, thou shalt die.[34]

Even though Jesus had predicted his resurrection, his disciples did not believe it initially. The Gospel of Matthew tells us that some of the disciples who met Jesus on the mountain in Galilee "doubted" (Matt. 28:17). Likewise Mark shows the angels calming the women who came to the tomb (Mark 16:7).

The Gospel of Luke tells us of the two disciples on the road to Emmaus who had given in to despair. Christ's crucifixion had so discouraged them that they had given up hope. We hear their discouragement when Jesus encountered them on the road as they said, "But we had hoped. . ." (Luke 24:21). The crucifixion had relegated their hopes to the past tense. Jesus, though, walked with them and taught them. Then they sensed their "hearts burning within" (Luke 24:32). Breaking bread, Jesus ultimately revealed his identity to them. Jesus opened their hearts, their eyes, and their minds to the story of his resurrection (Luke 24:31, 32, 45).

According to John's Gospel, Mary Magdalene saw Jesus first after his resurrection but did not immediately recognize him (John 20:15). Even when John outran Peter to the tomb and Peter barged in first, they did not fully comprehend what they saw (John 20:3–9). Jesus appeared to ten of the disciples, but Thomas was missing. Later, Thomas also exclaimed he would not believe unless he saw proof. Jesus came to Thomas, and Thomas confessed his faith, "My Lord and my God" (John 20:28).

Many in our world still live by the adage, *Seeing is believing.* The Gospel of John espouses the opposite, *Believing is seeing.* When we believe, then we see God's work in a whole new light.

How many saw the risen Jesus? In Paul's explanation of the gospel in a letter to Corinth, he explained that the gospel he had preached and the gospel that had saved his hearers culminated in the resurrection and Jesus' appearance "to more than five hundred of the brothers at the same time" (1 Cor. 15:6). Later still, the risen Lord Jesus revealed his identity to Paul on the road to Damascus (Acts 9:5; 1 Cor. 15:8). When Paul preached on Mars Hill in Athens, the intellectual center of the ancient world, his listeners were polite until he mentioned the resurrection. "When they heard about the resurrection from the dead, some of them sneered" (Acts 17:32).

How has the risen Lord revealed himself to you? On February 14, 2003, a bus full of senior adults and friends left Memorial Baptist Church in Temple, Texas, and headed toward Dallas, Texas, to attend a concert. A heavy downpour and a slick highway resulted in a terrible tragedy. The bus careened across the median and struck another vehicle. In all, five from the bus and two from the passenger vehicle lost their lives.

My wife Melanie and I were packing for a mission trip to Poland when we received the phone call. Her parents were on the bus. Racing down the stairs, we turned on the television to see pictures of a bus on its side in the rain. We frantically called the local hospitals, trying to get any news about the tragedy. Finally we received a call from a Baptist chaplain in Temple telling us that Melanie's father Jim Freeman had survived but her mother Jo had died at the scene. Jo Freeman was a great follower of Jesus Christ. Years before, she had prevailed on me to promise to preach her funeral when she went to be with the Lord. I had no idea how hard it would be, but I kept my promise to her.

Some weeks later, on Easter Sunday, I preached from Mark's Gospel about the resurrection. It occurred to me that Jesus' promise spoken by the angel still stood, "He is going ahead of you into Galilee. There you will see him, just as he told you" (Mark 16:7). I invited the congregation to look for Jesus as he preceded them wherever they went that week. I was convinced that if we looked for Jesus in the neighborhood or at work, we would discover that he was already there.

After church, we put our sons in the car and made the trip to Temple to see Jim, Melanie's dad. Our youngest son, Chase, asked whether we could go to the cemetery. As a pastor, I rarely return to the burial sites of our members, although I know their families do. This day, I experienced a different sense of mourning as I walked where many others do.

When we arrived, we discovered the grass had not yet covered the brown patch of earth over the grave. The cloudy skies mirrored our emotions that day. All was dark and dismal. I was unprepared for the emotion I felt as I realized the scope of our loss. Unanticipated waves of grief came over me as I turned to walk away from the site. Then, seemingly out of nowhere, I heard music. In the distance a family gathered at a burial ceremony began to sing,

> When peace, like a river, attendeth my way,
> When sorrows like sea billows roll;
> Whatever my lot, Thou hast taught me to say,
> It is well, it is well with my soul.[35]

I turned to see the source of the singing and realized my sermon had been for myself that morning. I looked for Jesus, and he was there. Even in the cemetery, our Savior has preceded us and overcome the nightmare we call death. If Jesus goes before us into death and life, then where in this world is he not with us? "Where O death is your victory? Where O death is your sting?" (1 Cor. 15:55).

No matter how great our loss—even when we are at a loss or we are lost—our Father will find us. He sent his Son to seek and to save us.

Remember John Newton's words, "I once was lost, but now am found."[36] In Jesus we have been found. Are we willing to follow the One who has found us?

CHAPTER *Four*

Conversion

The Experience of Salvation

"I am not ashamed of the gospel, because it is
the power of God for the salvation of everyone
who believes, first for the Jew, then for the
Gentile. For in the gospel a righteousness
from God is revealed, a righteousness that
is by faith from first to last, just as it is
written: 'The righteous will live by faith.'"

—ROMANS 1:16–17

"Everyone who calls on the name
of the Lord will be saved."

—ROMANS 10:13

NOW THAT WE HAVE SEEN what God has done to save us, how do
we enter into this salvation? How does a person experience
the salvation God has so graciously provided?

Do you remember when you became a Christian? Sometimes in
revival meetings in the churches of my childhood, we identified the
day of the week on which we became Christians with this simple song:
"It was on a Monday . . . I saw the Light."

When and how does conversion take place? It is easier to discern the moment of Paul's conversion than Simon Peter's. Looking at Peter's story in the biblical narratives, when was Peter converted?[1] First, Andrew brought Peter to Jesus and told Peter Jesus was the Messiah (John 1:41–42). Later, Peter accepted Jesus' call after Jesus said, ". . . From now on you will catch men" (Luke 5:11). At Caesarea Philippi, Peter articulated a deeper faith by seeing and saying that Jesus was "the Christ" (Matthew 16:16). After his threefold denial of Jesus, Peter received a new invitation to love Christ and feed his sheep (John 21:15–19). On which of those occasions did Peter become a Christian?

Peter's story is not unlike our own. Baptists have often focused on salvation as a specific point in time, seeking to understand an exact time and place when and where one once and for all became a follower of Christ. The Apostle Paul's conversion confirms the possibility of salvation beginning in one dramatic moment (Acts 9:1–9). Is Paul's experience necessarily normative, however? As in Peter's story, salvation can involve a process by which we not only encounter Christ but also choose to follow him, understand who he is, and ultimately serve him. Likely, no one person's experience of salvation will prove to be the template for all people's experience.

Salvation certainly involves more than a formula and a prayer. Nevertheless, we do well to speak of a moment when a person is saved.[2] Salvation begins with a transaction, continues as a lifetime process, and culminates with a glorious consummation.

Conversion requires a conscious decision to follow Jesus Christ. No one can make such a decision for another person. Even our best intentions and efforts to bring our children into relationship with Christ are in vain unless the children consciously make their own commitment to Christ. Historians tell us of compulsory conversions of whole people groups enforced by conquerors or mandated by rulers. Such conversions do not amount to genuine commitments to Christ. Further, one is not a Christian because one is baptized legally into a state-sponsored church.

Commitment to Christ is ultimately a matter of the will. We can choose Christ as did the man healed of blindness (John 9:36–38) or reject him as did the rich young ruler (Mark 10:17–22).

Calvin Miller articulates our need for a conscious choice in his book *The Singer.* When somebody asked God, "Can you be merciful and send me off to hell and lock me in forever?" God replied, "No, pilgrim, I will not send you there, but if you chose to go there, I could never lock you out."[3]

Our personal experience of salvation, which we may term *conversion,* begins with conviction of sin. We cannot experience God's gift of salvation if we do not first understand and believe we need to be forgiven. In fact, Jesus' first sermon perfectly mirrored John the Baptist's first sermon. John came preaching, "Repent, for the kingdom of heaven is near" (Matthew 3:2). After Jesus heard of John's imprisonment, Jesus began to preach, "Repent, for the kingdom of heaven is near" (Matt. 4:17).

When God reveals his presence to us and all heaven breaks loose in our world, we experience conviction. Conviction may lead to repentance and ultimately to conversion.

Conviction of Sin

Salvation begins with conviction of sin. We must not confuse conviction with perpetual guilt or an oversensitive conscience. True conviction consists of an awareness of sin leading to sorrow and brokenness in the life of a person. Jesus promised conviction as the work of the Holy Spirit, "When he comes, he will convict the world of guilt in regard to sin and righteousness and judgment: in regard to sin because men do not believe in me. . ." (John 16:8). At times, the Spirit uses others in our lives to bring about this sense of conviction. In 2 Corinthians, Paul recalled how his previous painful letter created sorrow in the hearts of the believers in Corinth (2 Corinthians 7:7–9). The deep sorrow Paul caused the Corinthian believers served a temporary purpose and gave way to joy. Because God intended the sorrow, the believers were not harmed by it. Paul explained, "Godly sorrow brings repentance that leads to salvation and leaves no regret" (2 Cor. 7:10). In contrast to worldly sorrow, which leads to death, godly sorrow or conviction leads to life.

The Scriptures offer numerous examples of conviction. Beginning with the story of Adam and Eve hiding from God after their disobedience, we learn that when unholy people encounter the holy God, they become deeply aware of their sinfulness (Genesis 3). Later, David expressed his conviction and ours when he wrote, "For I know my transgressions, and my sin is always before me. Against you, you only, have I sinned and done what is evil in your sight, so that you are proved right when you speak and justified when you judge" (Psalm 51:3–4).

In the Old Testament story of Isaiah's encounter with God in the temple, the prophet saw God as God really is, "high and exalted," "filling the temple" (Isaiah 6:1). In this multi-sensory experience of worship, Isaiah heard the voices of the seraphim echoing off the walls, resounding in the chambers of his own heart, "Holy, holy, holy is the LORD God Almighty, the whole earth is full of his glory" (Isa. 6:3). Immediately, Isaiah recognized an important truth about God. First, God is "holy," meaning *other*, or *of a different kind*. In fact, the repetition of the words resounding in Isaiah's ears reveals that God is more than just a little holy. He is completely, utterly, perfectly holy. In addition, Isaiah realized this holy God is inescapable. Not only does God fill the temple, but also God's glory fills the earth.

As surely as Isaiah saw God's holiness, he recognized his own unholiness. "'Woe to me!' I cried. 'I am ruined! For I am a man of unclean lips, and I live among a people of unclean lips, and my eyes have seen the King, the LORD Almighty" (Isa. 6:5). Conviction arrested Isaiah. The immortal God immobilized him. In Isaiah's own words, he was undone, disintegrating. Why? Because he was a man of unclean lips and he lived among a people of unclean lips. God's holiness convicted Isaiah of the unholiness of his speech and his people's speech. When we encounter a holy God and see ourselves as we really are, we recognize that something must change for us to be right with God.

Luke tells a similar story in the New Testament (Luke 5:1–11). Simon Peter first heard about Jesus through Andrew his brother (John 1:40–42). In the days that followed, Peter had to discover for himself that Jesus was the Messiah. Surrounded by the crowds, Jesus sat in Simon's boat and taught the people. When Jesus had finished teaching, Jesus told Simon to fish again. Although Simon had fished all night unsuccessfully, he reluctantly obeyed and caught a miraculous number of fish. At that moment, Simon recognized he had met the Master; he felt the depths of his own sinfulness. Listen to his words, "Go away from me, Lord; I am a sinful man" (Luke 5:8). One might think that an entrepreneurial spirit like Simon Peter would seize on the opportunity to become a wealthy fisherman with Jesus' help. Not so. The compelling Christ convicted Peter of his sinfulness.

C. S. Lewis's description of the beginning of his own conversion bears a striking resemblance to Peter's stories.

> You must picture me alone in [my] room . . . night after night, feeling, whenever my mind lifted even for a second from my work, the steady, unrelenting approach of Him whom I so earnestly desired not to meet. That which I greatly feared had at last come upon me. In 1929 I gave in, and admitted that God was God, and knelt and prayed: perhaps, that night, the most dejected and reluctant convert in all England. I did not then see what is now the most shining thing; the Divine humility which will accept a convert even on such terms. The prodigal son at least walked home on his own feet. But who can duly adore that Love which will open the high gates to a prodigal who is brought in kicking, struggling, resentful, and darting his eyes in every direction for a chance to escape?[4]

The experiences of Peter and Paul speak to us about conviction of sin. Peter followed Jesus' trials at a seemingly safe distance. Given the chance to acknowledge his relationship with Jesus, Peter chose instead to deny Jesus three times. After the third time, Jesus turned and looked at him, causing Peter to go out and weep bitterly (Luke 22:60–62). Later, three times Jesus asked Peter whether he loved him. Peter finally answered, "Lord, you know all things" (John 21:15–19). Peter's conviction in light of his sin prepared him to proclaim Christ at Pentecost. The reaction of the crowd mirrored Peter's response on encountering Jesus, "When the people heard this, they were cut to the heart and said to Peter and the other apostles, 'Brothers what shall we do?'" (Acts 2:37). Peter's command to repent demonstrates that the crowd had been convicted of sin but had not yet acted on that conviction.

Later when Paul encountered the risen Lord on the road to Damascus in a dazzling, blinding light, he asked for an explanation of his own sin and received it (Acts 9:5). Reflecting on his prior persecution of Jesus' followers, Paul described himself as the "the worst" of sinners (1 Timothy 1:15).

In these examples, we learn not only the nature of conviction but also the source of conviction. Through an encounter with the holy God of heaven, sinners recognize that we are unholy. So God alone brings conviction in the life of a sinner.

How does God bring conviction? Through the proclamation of the Scriptures, the people at Pentecost were "cut to the heart" (Acts 2:37). In the Old Testament, the prophet Nathan confronted David's sin with Bathsheba by speaking the timeless words, "You are the man" (2 Samuel 12:7).

Further, at the end of the Old Testament, the prophet Malachi remembered the exemplary priest from the tribe of Levi "who turned many from their sin" (Malachi 2:6). This conviction emanated from the priest's teaching and example. The New Testament fulfills this teaching through the idea of the priesthood of every believer (1 Peter 2:4, 9; Revelation 1:6). As priests to each other, we can live our lives and proclaim God's truth in ways that bring genuine conviction. This ministry bears fruit: "My brothers if one of you should wander from the truth and someone should bring him back, remember this: Whoever turns a sinner from the error of his way will save him from death and cover over a multitude of sins" (James 5:20). The proclamation of the gospel, empowered by God's Holy Spirit, brings a person to the place of readiness for repentance and faith.

Repentance from Sin

Two deacons alternated in prayer each week at their church. One deacon prayed the same prayer each time, "Lord, clean out the cobwebs from the windowsills of our hearts." While some found the prayer to be eloquent and expressive of their hearts, the second deacon was irritated both by the redundancy and by what this second

deacon perceived to be the inaccuracy of the other deacon's theology.
One Sunday the second deacon could take it no more. He interrupted the fellow deacon's prayer by saying, "Lord, don't do it. Kill
the spider!" If our understanding of salvation does not lead to the
death of sin in our lives, we have misunderstood the New Testament
idea of repentance.

One of my fellow ministers recently welcomed guests in our worship service by inviting everyone present to complete our guest card,
saying, "We want our members to complete the information as well
because perhaps you have changed your address or e-mail address, or
maybe you've changed your phone number." And then he appealed,
"If you've changed anything in your life, please, write it down on this
sheet of paper." Repentance requires a radical reorientation of life
and values, resulting in transformation and conversion.

The Hebrew term in the Old Testament for repentance is *shub*,
which means *to turn* or *return*. The New Testament, written in Greek,
uses two words to convey repentance. *Epistrepho* captures an idea
similar to the Old Testament *shub*, referring to a *turning of the will to
God* and *a returning to the Savior*. *Metanoeo* conveys the thought of *a
change of mind*.[5] To what shall our minds change? "Let this mind be
in you, which was also in Christ Jesus. . ." (Philippians 2:5, KJV). Once
we change our minds, we regret the previous course of action, and we
resolve to live differently.

One might respond to the revelation of God's presence in any
number of ways. Not everyone repents. When Jesus told the rich ruler
the truth and instructed him to sell his possessions, give to the poor,
and follow him, the man went away sad, unwilling to divest himself
of his considerable wealth (Mark 10:17–22). His sadness did not con-
stitute real repentance because it did not result in any change in his
life. But to become a Christian, one must to come to repentance.

Consider another snapshot from Jesus' ministry. The Gospel of
Luke tells the story of Zacchaeus, the tax collector who had become
wealthy by defrauding others of their wealth (Luke 19:1–10). At the
moment when Jesus urged Zacchaeus to descend from the tree and
invited himself to supper at Zacchaeus's house, the people began
to mutter, "He has gone to be the guest of a 'sinner'" (Luke 19:7).

Zacchaeus's confession revealed the beginning of his transformation, "Look, Lord! Here and now I give half of my possessions to the poor and if I have cheated anybody out of anything, I will pay back four times the amount" (Luke 19:8). This radical reversal constituted repentance. Zacchaeus not only ceased to steal from others but wished to repay what he had stolen.

Jesus' words at this point speak volumes. "Today salvation has come to this house, for this man, too, is a son of Abraham. For the Son of Man came to seek and to save what was lost" (Luke 19:10). Zacchaeus had been lost to God and culpable in the eyes of the people. But when he looked for Jesus, Jesus found him. The presence of Christ prompted a change of mind, which led to a change of behavior. We come to repentance in the same way.

In repentance we put to death our love of sin.[6] So repentance is more than just feeling sorry for mistakes one has made or being upset about having been caught in sin.

Our first response to conviction may be regret over the consequences of our actions without accepting responsibility. The story is told of an unbeliever who went to seek spiritual counsel from a pastor. When the pastor heard his story he asked him, "Are you sorry for what you have done?"

The man answered honestly, "No, I cannot say that I am."

They seemed to be at an impasse until the pastor pressed further. "Are you sorry that you are not sorry?"

After an agonizing moment, the dam burst, and the flood gates broke in the man's soul. "Yes. I am sorry that I am not sorry," he confessed. This was the beginning of repentance for him.

When we repent, we feel so sorry that we consciously reject our past sinful behavior. We change our minds about sin.

On a trip to New York City, our family used the subway system to travel around the city. At one point we boarded a train headed the wrong direction. A New Yorker overheard our conversation and our confusion. He kindly encouraged us to exit the train at the next stop and take another train in the opposite direction. Had we stayed on the train going north we would never have arrived at our destination to the south. Similarly, before we meet Christ we are headed in the wrong direction. When we meet Christ, he invites us to *change trains* and head in the opposite direction. This is repentance.

Our repentance is not just a momentary event, never to be repeated. When we truly repent, we live lives of repentance. Having died to sin, we put that death into practice (Romans 6:2, 11). Such repentance is not the same as confession of sin, but it leads to it. The Greek word for *confess* is *homologeo*, which literally means *to say the same thing* or *to agree*. When we confess, we are simply agreeing with God, who says that we have all sinned.

One of our favorite basketball players is Dikembe Mutombo, who completed his professional career with the Houston Rockets. He is a strong Christian who has greatly helped the people of his home country, the Democratic Republic of the Congo, by establishing a hospital, largely with his own donations. An outstanding defensive player, Mutombo made it difficult for the other team to score. Some time ago, a local news broadcast chronicled the expressions on Dikembe's face when the referees called a foul on him. Although some players immediately raise a hand to acknowledge their fouls, Dikembe typically raised both hands and expresses disbelief. As one of his teammates put it, "Dikembe does not believe that he has ever committed a foul." Of course he knows he has, but in the heat of the moment, he is reluctant to admit it. This approach may represent a good strategy to remain in the game, but it would be a poor spiritual strategy for our relationships with God. "If we claim we have not sinned, we make God out to be a liar and his word has no place in our lives" (1 John 1:10).

In some traditions, people confess to their priest or minister. To whom should we confess as followers of Christ? "If we confess our sins to him, God is faithful to forgive us and to cleanse us from all unrighteousness" (1 John 1:9). First, our confession is made to God. Jesus Christ, our great High Priest, is our mediator (Heb. 9:15). This is not to say that we bear no accountability to others at all. In fact, James invites us, "Therefore confess your sins to each other. . ." (James 5:16). The priesthood of every believer remains one of the distinctive teachings of Baptists. Every believer in Christ is a priest to others. We represent one another to God when we pray for one another.

Simultaneously, we represent God to one another through proclamation of the truth.

What should we confess? We should confess our own sins. It is easy to notice and confess the sins of others. In fact, we can be hard on others who sin, deeming their mistakes as worse than our own. In England I encountered a beautiful prayer as the people received the Lord's Supper, "We do not presume to come to this your table, merciful Lord, trusting in our own righteousness, but in your manifold and great mercies. We are not worthy so much as to gather up the crumbs under your table."

Faith in Christ

Jesus added a call to "believe" to John the Baptist's call to "repent" (compare Mark 1:4, 15). In Greek, *believe* is the verbal form for the noun *faith*.[7] Our word *trust* captures the essence of the word for faith and belief.[8] "Faith is so uniquely central to Christianity that it may properly define Christianity's essence."[9] We experience God's salvation by believing or placing our trust in Christ. When Nicodemus came to Jesus by night, Jesus said, "For God so loved the world that he gave his one and only Son that whoever believes in him shall not perish but have eternal life" (John 3:16).

Theologians speak of three important components to our faith. First we must know, then we must assent to the truth we know, and ultimately we must place our trust in Christ.[10] In my office, I have a favorite chair in which I sit to read and pray. I know this chair will hold me, and I even give assent to that fact. But in order to get the benefit of the chair I must move beyond knowledge and assent to trust that the chair will hold me. Ultimately I must sit in the chair to enjoy it.

How do we make the leap of faith? Even our faith comes by God's grace according to Paul. "For it is by grace you have been saved, through faith—and this not from yourselves, it is the gift of God—not by works so that no one can boast" (Ephesians 2:8–9). Our ability to trust owes to God alone. Still, we must consciously and willingly place our trust in Christ in order to be saved. As someone has suggested, "God doesn't have any grandchildren, only children."[11] Each individual soul must believe in Christ in order to experience salvation.

In Paul's Letter to the Romans, he made the case that salvation is always given exclusively by means of faith. He wrote, "Abraham believed God, and it was credited to him as righteousness" (Rom. 4:3; see Genesis 15:6). Certainly, as the Book of James teaches, saving faith results in works, but salvation comes by faith and not by works (James 2:14–24).

Who is the object of our faith? Salvation comes through faith in Christ alone. We believe *in* Christ. In fact, the word "in" in John 3:16 comes from the Greek preposition *eis*, which is often translated *into*. The expression suggests a deep intimacy and confidence.

What about people who have never heard of Jesus? Are they lost for eternity? People ask me this question frequently. My first response is that for people like us who have access to the gospel, the answer is clear: we must believe in Christ.

What about those who do not have access to the gospel? At one level, everyone has access to God. Paul wrote about the wrath of God being "revealed from heaven against all the godlessness and wickedness of men, who suppress the truth by their wickedness, *since what may be known about God is plain to them, because God has made it plain to them*" (Rom.1:18–19, italics added for emphasis). He continued, "For since the creation of the world God's invisible qualities—his eternal power and divine nature—have been clearly seen, being understood from what has been made, so that men are without excuse" (Rom. 1:20). We are responsible for the light we have, and we all have enough light to know that God is there. Still, having this amount of light is not the same as having the gospel story available to us.

One friend in our church who grew up in another culture asked about her grandparents and great-grandparents who had no access to the gospel. "Will they be in heaven?" she wondered. The universalist answers this by saying, "Everyone will be in heaven." But the Scriptures teach that Jesus is the way, the truth, and the life. No one comes to the Father except through him (John 14:6).

Bible interpreter Christopher Wright has proposed that people without access to Christ may still be saved through Christ without knowing specifically what Christ has done for them. He states, "God will save through Christ some who even though they never hear about Christ in their earthly lifetimes, nevertheless turn to God in some kind of repentance and faith."[12] He points out that some Old Testament believers, like Abraham, never knew about the historical Jesus of Nazareth. They were saved by Christ (whose death is effective for all human history) but not through knowing Christ. Wright extends this to non-Israelite believers like Rahab, Ruth, Naaman, and the Ninevites converted by Jonah's preaching. Wright quickly distinguishes this from universalism or from saying that good and sincere people of any faith earn their way to heaven by practicing their own rituals.

Whatever the possibilities for Wright's proposal as a whole, he is certainly correct that people can be saved only through Christ. Perhaps it is beyond our ability to know what God will do ultimately for those who because of history or geography never hear about Jesus but choose to repent and trust in God. At the end of the day, as Wright says, we must let God be God. Simultaneously we must be the church. This very fact places a great urgency on the church to tell the story of the gospel in evangelism and missions.

What exactly must one believe to experience salvation? James helps us see that belief in the existence of God is not enough. "You believe that there is one God. Good! Even the demons believe that—and shudder" (James 2:19). John 3:16 says we must believe in Jesus to access eternal life. More specifically, Paul affirmed that one must believe in one's heart that God raised Christ from the dead in order to be saved (Rom. 10:9). Only when we believe in the resurrection can we appropriate the salvation Christ offers.

Where does faith occur? Is it a mere matter of cognitive, intellectual assent? Paul explained, "For it is with your heart that you believe and are justified" (Rom. 10:10). Here we see the heart as the center of the will. We must volitionally choose to place our faith in Christ as our Savior and Lord.

The beginning of the great chapter of faith in Hebrews defines saving faith like this: "Faith is being sure of what we hope for and certain of what we do not see" (Heb. 11:1). Jesus told Thomas, "Because you have seen me, you have believed; blessed are those who have not seen and yet have believed" (John 20:29).

Confession of Christ as Lord

A wealthy Texas oil engineer sent his uncle and aunt a rare bird for Christmas. Calling to see whether it had arrived, he asked his uncle, a simple country farmer, "How did you like the bird?"

"It was delicious," he responded.

Flustered, the nephew said, "You don't mean you ate that bird. It cost me a fortune. That bird had learned to speak five languages fluently."

"Well," the uncle responded, "then he should have said something."

Our faith is a verbal faith. "Let the redeemed of the LORD say so. . ." (Psalm 107:2).

We may wrongly associate confession as exclusively related to sin. Although we learn in the Scriptures to confess our sin, we become Christians by confessing our Savior. Paul explains, "That if you confess with your mouth, 'Jesus is Lord,' and believe in your heart that God raised him from the dead, you will be saved" (Rom. 10:9).

The Gospel of John contains a number of important confessions of faith. On meeting Jesus and realizing that Jesus already knew him, Nathanael confessed, "Rabbi, you are the Son of God; you are the King of Israel" (John 1:49). After the blind man was healed, he confessed, "Lord, I believe" (John 9:38). Martha said, "Yes, Lord, I believe that you are the Christ, the Son of God, who was to come into the world" (John 11:27). Exhilarated by an encounter with the risen Lord, Mary Magdalene confessed, "I have seen the Lord!" (John 20:18). When Christ vanquished his doubt, Thomas confessed, "My Lord and my God!" (John 20:28).[13]

Christians confess or profess their faith publicly. Jesus said, "Whoever acknowledges me before men, I will also acknowledge him before my Father in heaven" (Matt. 10:32). Peter made his great confession in the presence of the disciples at Caesarea Philippi, saying, "You are the Christ, the Son of the living God" (Matt. 16:16).

In David Barrett's *World Encyclopedia of Christianity*, he uses the intriguing expression *Crypto-Christians* to describe secret believers in countries that oppress followers of Christ.[14] The term is not as frightening as it sounds. The word *crypto* is derived from a Greek word that means *hidden* or *secret*. Sometimes a person says about his or her faith, *It is a very private matter for me*. Undoubtedly, the Christian faith calls for a profound personal commitment to Christ, but this commitment should not remain a secret.

In Nicodemus's story we find an example of one who was fascinated with Jesus as a teacher. When Nicodemus "came to Jesus at night" (John 3:2), Jesus called him to emerge from the darkness into the light. John 3:21 states, "Whoever lives by the truth comes into the light. . . ." Nicodemus's silence in the text is deafening. Later when he started to speak up for Jesus before the Pharisees, they asked him, "Are you from Galilee, too?" (John 7:52). Again Nicodemus remained private with his convictions. Perhaps Nicodemus is included with the spiritual leaders who "would not confess their faith for fear that they would be put out of the synagogue; for they loved praise from men more than praise from God" (John 12:42–43). Again Jesus called for public commitment, "I have come into the world as a light, so that no one who believes in me should stay in the darkness" (John 12:46). Only after Jesus was crucified did Nicodemus find the courage to acknowledge publicly his allegiance to Jesus (John 19:39).

How are we as Baptists confessing Christ in the context of our worship? Often at the time of the invitation, the new believer is silent as the minister prays for him or her. Then in the baptistery, the minister speaks. The new believer is asked to respond only with a simple *yes* or *no*, if that, to a question about salvation. As a result, the new believer has scant opportunity to confess his or her faith publicly. We must offer new believers the opportunity to express the decisions they are making for Christ.

Not only in worship services but in worshipful lives we profess our faith and confess our relationship to Christ. Everyone who knows us ought to know about our commitment to Christ. Jesus challenges us with these words, "Whoever acknowledges me before men, I will also acknowledge him before my Father in heaven. But whoever disowns me before men, I will disown him before my Father in heaven" (Matthew 10:32–33).

Some years ago, my grandfather, who lived in the state of Washington, called my father and asked him whether I could come and talk to him about the Lord. My grandfather was on kidney dialysis at the time and did not know how long he would live. I met my dad in Washington, and we made the scenic drive through the Columbia River Gorge up to the Yakima Valley.

My grandfather had made a lot of admittedly poor choices in his earlier life, and he was ready to consider his relationship with God. We sat down outside in the shade of a tree and talked about the way to receive Christ. He acknowledged his need. We joined in prayer as he invited Christ into his life.

A few weeks later, he went down to the little Baptist church in his town and followed the Lord in believer's baptism by immersion. Later, a family member asked me whether it is ever too late to become a Christian. I responded that as long as we are alive, we have the opportunity to follow Christ. It is not too late. Neither is it too early!

CHAPTER Five

A New You

"Therefore if anyone is in Christ, he is a new
creation; the old has gone, the new has come!"

—2 CORINTHIANS 5:17

PHYSICALLY IMPOSING, MY FRIEND DWIGHT possessed both the size and the agility to play as a lineman for a major college football program. Instead, Dwight chose to stay home on the farm and raise cattle, in deference to a father more committed to work than to what he considered the foolishness of football. Over time, Dwight gained the respect of other ranchers by working at cattle auctions in several of the small towns of central Texas. All the while, his godly mother prayed for him to become a Christian.

One summer, in preparing for our church's revival services, we prayed fervently for Dwight in the weeks leading up to the revival. During the week, we noticed his truck at his parents' house and dropped by, but he went out the back door before we could talk. Many in the church intensified their prayer efforts, asking that Dwight might come to Christ. I will never forget the night he came to the meeting, walked down the aisle, and professed his faith in Christ.

The next weekend old friends invited him to join them in old activities. Dwight said, "I am not the person I used to be." As the years have progressed, so has Dwight in his faith. He has served as a lay preacher in his local church, filling in when his pastor is way. Those who knew Dwight before wondered what happened to him. His Christian friends recognized that the one who makes "the new" to come had transformed him and given him a new life.

Regeneration: God Gives Us Life

What happens in the life of a believer when he or she receives Christ? I grew up in churches that sometimes reduced salvation to the promise that we will live in heaven when we die. The New Testament teaches us there is more, much more to salvation than a fire insurance policy out of hell and a free ticket to heaven.

A constellation of beautiful words describes the multifaceted dimensions of salvation. First, Christianity offers each person *a new birth.* When Nicodemus complimented Jesus as a teacher from God and a worker of miracles, Jesus responded, "I tell you the truth, no one can see the kingdom of God unless he is born again" (John 3:3). Dumbfounded, Nicodemus, a Pharisee and member of the Jewish ruling council, asked, "How can a man be born when he is old?" (John 3:4). Without hesitating, Jesus distinguished spiritual rebirth from physical birth, saying, ". . . No one can enter the kingdom of God unless he is born of water and the Spirit" (John 3:5–6). A third time, Jesus applied this to Nicodemus specifically, stating, "You must be born again" (John 3:7–8).

New life is not merely metaphorical or hypothetical for believers. The Apostle Paul shed light on this concept in his anguished letter to the Galatians, "My dear children, for whom I am again in the pains of childbirth until Christ is formed in you" (Galatians 4:19). Paul labored over the Galatians because he wanted a new birth for them.

This spiritual rebirth involves an inward spiritual formation through which Christ himself is formed in the believer. Even creation groans in labor, waiting "for the sons of God to be revealed" (Romans 8:19–22).

Thankfully, Christians are born anew to "a living hope" (1 Peter 1:3). This emphasis on new birth has long distinguished Baptists. We do not believe that one becomes a Christian simply because his or her parents or grandparents were Christians. Just as a person must be born to experience life, so a person must be born again spiritually to become right with God.

We may be as confused about this as Nicodemus was. For all of our familiarity with the idea of *born-again* Christianity, we may misunderstand the theological import of the term. Only the Spirit of God can give a person a new beginning. Just as the wind appears to have a mind of its own, similarly one cannot predict the regenerative work of the Holy Spirit. Jesus said to Nicodemus, "The wind blows wherever it pleases. . . . So it is with everyone born of the Spirit" (John 3:8).

Living along the Texas coast has awakened me to the unpredictability and awesome power of the wind. Earlier, as a student pastor, I watched the awful impact of tornadoes spun off by Hurricane Alicia in Central Texas. More recently, we have seen the devastating effects of hurricanes hitting in the Beaumont area. My family ran from Hurricane Rita with a million of our closest neighbors. Our normal three-hour trip from Houston to our family in Temple, Texas, lasted more than sixteen hours that day. Had not the storm turned in its last hours, our home would have been hit.

We did not dodge Hurricane Ike when it hit Galveston and moved through Houston. A pastor friend who has served in Galveston for more than twenty years stayed with members in his church. Together they watched the water rising under the pulpit and inflicting severe water damage to their historic building. At our own church, winds of more than 100 miles per hour peeled back the roof on our sanctuary like it was a tin can. With gratitude to meteorologists, we must confess that our twenty centuries of technological advances have still left us powerless to predict or harness the wind.

We are thankful that the wind of God's Spirit builds instead of destroys. The Spirit brings life, not death. In May of 1997, when severe tornadoes touched down in Central Texas, devastating the town of Jarrell, a category F–3 tornado came through Cedar Park where we lived. I saw the funnel cloud from the front door of our church offices, and I headed home, barely arriving before the storm hit our neighborhood. Although our home was spared, many in our neighborhood lost everything. As Texas Baptist Men came and served food to the community, my wife and I had the chance to listen to the stories of our neighbors. Two elementary-age boys, Kenny and Robbie Entrekin, members of New Hope Baptist Church, were home alone when the tornado shifted their house. After the wind subsided, they raced to the backyard to check on their pet rabbit. It had lived in a cage attached to their garage. The cage was gone. Imagine two young boys walking through the neighborhood looking for their pet.

Just then a neighbor across the street asked, "Are you looking for a rabbit?

"Yes," they answered tremulously.

"Well, he is in my living room."

The storm had lifted the cage containing the rabbit, carried it across the street and through the neighbor's window, and deposited it in her living room. The apparently unharmed rabbit was named *Zippy*.

The wind often evokes fear, but the wind of God's Spirit calls for our faith. God offers us hope, not harm.

The Old Testament prophet Ezekiel tells the story of dry bones on a valley floor being brought to life by "breath" entering into them (Ezekiel 37:8). "Breath" is *ruach*, the Hebrew word for wind or breath or spirit). Ezekiel lived in a time of geographic and spiritual exile. In that time in Israel's history, the people of Israel felt as though they were dead because they were cut off from their homes and homeland and worst of all cut off from hope. God wanted to impart the hope of new life, and so he gave Ezekiel a vision of death passing into life. Showing Ezekiel a valley full of dry bones, scattered abroad, God asked, "Can these bones live?" Ezekiel answered, "O Sovereign LORD, you alone know" (Ezekiel 37:3). God's answer was for Ezekiel to preach to the bones. When the prophet obeyed, the bones came together, covered with sinews and skin; but still "there was no breath in them" (Ezek. 37:8). Then God told Ezekiel to preach again, this time to the *ruach*, the Hebrew word for wind or breath or spirit. Now the bones "came to life and stood up on their feet—a vast army" (Ezek. 37:9–10).

Only the power of the Spirit could bring them to life. God concluded, "O my people, I am going to open your graves and bring you up from them; I will bring you back to the land of Israel. Then you, my people, will know that I am the Lord, when I open your graves and bring you up from them. I will put my Spirit in you and you will live" (Ezek. 37:12–14).

From time to time, I teach a homiletics course at Houston Baptist University. One day just before Easter, I took my students on a field trip. Although they all wanted to know where we were going, I kept our destination secret, instructing them to bring their Bibles and to come prepared to preach. After we loaded into the van, they began to speculate about where we were going.

"Are we going to the mall?"

"No," I answered.

We approached a penitentiary. "Are we preaching there?"

"No."

"We can't just go and preach at a public school."

"I know," I answered. Then I pulled up beside a cemetery just behind a neighborhood in Southwest Houston. The students looked at me skeptically as I stopped the van and stepped out. I motioned for them to follow, and we stopped in front of a tombstone. I said, "Preach to the people who are buried here. What do you have to say to them?"

One zealous young pastor broke the uneasy silence, shouting in a beautiful timbre, "It is too late for you people. You should have made your decision before you died."

Sharing the story of Ezekiel 37, I showed them that we must finally depend on the Spirit to bring people to life. It is not enough to perceive the problem of spiritual death, by agreeing with Paul, "You were dead in your transgressions and sins. . ." (Ephesians 2:1). We must finally proclaim the power of spiritual life, trusting God's resurrection power to lift our listeners to life.

Jesus Christ did not come to make bad people good. He came to make dead people live. In the New Testament, Paul personalized and applied the power of resurrection to the church at Corinth, "By his power God raised the Lord from the dead, and he will raise us also" (1 Corinthians 6:14).

Paul also wrote, "And if the Spirit of him who raised Christ from the dead is living in you, he who raised Christ from the dead will also give life to your mortal bodies through his Spirit who lives in you" (Romans 8:11). What does it mean to have Christ formed in us, living inside of us through the Holy Spirit? If a Hall of Fame baseball pitcher lived in me, I could throw a fastball. If a champion tennis player lived inside me, I could play tennis. If a champion golfer lived inside of me, I could play golf. Because the risen Lord Jesus Christ lives inside us, we can live victoriously.

Paul offered the expression "new creation" (2 Cor. 5:17) as another metaphor for the new life of the regenerated believer. When God created humankind, God pronounced creation "very good" (Genesis 1:31). As we have seen, sin seriously disrupted God's ideal for humankind. Through Christ, however, God's image for human-kind finds restoration. Paul expressed it this way, "If any person is in Christ, he becomes a new creation; the old has gone, the new has come!" (2 Cor. 5:17).

In the process of regeneration, God removes our sin, guilt, and shame. For the believers in Galatia, this meant an end to their legalis-tic observance of the law as a way to please God. "Neither circumcision nor uncircumcision means anything; what counts is a new creation" (Galatians 6:15). We no longer try to save ourselves, because Christ has taken away the false idea that we could earn salvation by keeping the Old Testament law.

God makes all things new in the lives of believers. Paul captured this thought in his powerful challenge to the believers in Rome, "Therefore, I urge you, brothers, in view of God's mercy, to offer your bodies as living sacrifices, holy and pleasing to God—this is your spiritual act of worship. Do not conform any longer to the pattern of this world, but be transformed by the renewing of your mind" (Rom. 12:1–2). Believers no longer offer the animal sacrifices prescribed in the Old Testament. Instead, we become living sacrifices. Neither do we conform to the old patterns of our sinful world, but instead we experience transformation. God renews our minds. When our thinking changes, our behavior follows.

Paul also used the word *justification* to describe the transaction of salvation. Justification is not merely forensic, not just a legal transaction. Rather, justification is another way of describing the new life we have in Christ.[1] Through Christ, God not only *counts* us right but *makes* us right.

Justification: God Makes Us Right

If parents can avoid it, they should never relocate children during their adolescent years. This sage advice has helped many families. In our military family, those words proved impossible to heed. We moved from Germany to Washington D. C., then back to Germany, and from there to Montana in a period of about five years while my older brothers and I were teens. The second greatest part of this culture shock was being a Dallas Cowboys' fan and having to live in Washington Redskin country for a year. What could be worse? What produced an even greater shock was moving from the disco culture of the military bases in Europe to the true cowboy culture of Montana. I had experienced vibrant Baptist churches in Texas, Alaska, Florida, Missouri, Illinois, Maryland, and Germany. But Montana provided a different spiritual landscape. It was a long way between towns and sometimes an even longer way between Baptist churches. I felt stranded in Big Sky Country. We did, however, connect with a number of other Baptists and also find allies in conservative Lutheran Christians. My Lutheran friends and I did not agree on everything, but in the doctrine of justification by grace through faith alone, we discovered common ground. The Protestant Reformation, I would later learn, started in part over this very issue: how can a person be made right with God?

"Justification involves a change of status in our relationship with God."[2] Justification means that God takes our part and undertakes our deliverance. He is for us rather than against us. In a sense, as long as we are against God, God is against us. But the moment we hear God's call and place our faith in him, God is for us. In the story of Abraham, even before the Mosaic law had been given, we discover that this great patriarch became right with God by simply believing God's promise to him. "Abraham believed the LORD, and he credited it to him as righteousness" (Genesis 15:6).

Of course we can never be innocent enough to justify ourselves before God. ". . . No one living is righteous before" God (Psalm 143:2). Our works will not suffice. ". . . They will not benefit you" (Isaiah 57:12).

How then are we made right with God? In the words David wrote after he sinned with Bathsheba, we find hope for justification. Not only is God justified when he judges us guilty of sin (Ps. 51:4). But our just God justifies us by his mercy and grace. "Have mercy on me, O God, according to your unfailing love; according to your great compassion blot out my transgressions" (Ps. 51:1). David knew what we must know: God cannot be appeased by the blood of animal sacrifices. "You do not delight in sacrifice, or I would bring it; you do not take pleasure in burnt offerings" (Ps. 51:16).[3]

In the New Testament, an expert in the law sought to justify himself by claiming to have completely kept the law (Luke 10:29). Others tried to justify themselves, too (Luke 16:15). But in Jesus' remarkable parable about the tax collector and the Pharisee, we learn that the wicked man who fell on God's mercy went down to his house justified instead of the religious leader who depended on his self-righteousness (Luke 18:14).

In his Letter to the Galatians, Paul was doing battle with false teachers who treated the law as a means to salvation. Not only did these Judaizers justify themselves by their own keeping of the law, but they also demanded that the Gentiles do the same. Paul clarified the inability of the law to justify us: "If righteousness could be gained through the law, Christ died for nothing" (Gal. 2:21). Paul contended that the Galatians were saved not by works of the law but by believing the gospel they heard.[4] Further, they received the Spirit not through the law but through faith (Gal. 3:5). As Abraham believed and was credited as righteous, so those who believe today are daughters and sons of Abraham (Gal. 3:6–9). Quoting the Old Testament prophet Habakkuk, Paul contended, "Clearly no one is justified before God by the law, because, 'The righteous will live by faith'" (Gal. 3:10).

Only God's perfect righteousness can satisfy God's holiness. The Apostle Paul wrote, "God made him who had no sin to become sin for us so that in him, we might become the righteousness of God" (2 Cor. 5:21). Christ alone possesses the power to justify us.

We owe our greatest debt to the Apostle Paul for his clear teaching on the subject of justification. How are we justified? Paul assured his readers that the works of the law will never justify us or make us right with God (see Rom. 3:20; 4:2; Gal. 2:16; 3:11; 5:4). Instead, he taught that we are "justified by grace through the redemption that came by Jesus Christ" (Rom. 3:24). God's grace, or *unmerited favor*, is our only hope. He demonstrates his grace through the redemption that came by Jesus Christ.

How did Christ redeem us? Because Christ was obedient to the cross (Rom. 5:19), we are "justified by his blood" (Rom. 5:9). We as sinners are the object of God's justification. God is the one who justifies us. "God presented [Jesus] as a sacrifice of atonement, through faith in his blood. He did this to demonstrate his justice . . . so as to be just and the one who justifies those who have faith in Jesus" (Rom. 3:24–25). We access this justification by placing our trust in Christ alone. Consequently, we experience the peace, joy, and hope of God's glory (Rom. 5:1–2).

Bible scholar N. T. Wright contends that God *makes* believers right as well as *counts* them right.[5] This approach significantly impacts the potential for spiritual growth. If God has empowered us and made us right, then we can begin to confirm the reality of our salvation by living right and setting wrongs in our world right. The same faith that accesses justification also empowers us to live.

Forgiveness: God Restores Relationship

Les Miserables, Victor Hugo's great novel, now a musical, tells the story of Jean Valjean, who served nineteen years in prison for stealing bread. Captivity hardened him. On Valjean's release, a kindly bishop was the only one who offered him a place to stay. During the night, Valjean rose to steal the bishop's silverware. When the bishop caught him, Valjean knocked him out and went on his way. The gendarmes caught Valjean, though. The next day the gendarmes came to return the silver and confirm the theft. But the bishop surprised the thief with grace, "'Ah! here you are!' he exclaimed, looking at Jean Valjean. 'I am glad to see you. Well, but how is this? I gave you the candlesticks too, which are of silver like the rest, and for which you can certainly get two hundred francs. Why did you not carry them away with your forks and spoons?'" Jean Valjean's eyes widened. He was now staring at the old man with an expression no words can convey. The bishop told the gendarmes the silver was a gift. As the gendarmes left, the bishop spoke to his mystified new friend Valjean these healing, redeeming words, "Do not forget, never forget, that you have promised to use the money in becoming an honest man." [6] Empowered by grace, Valjean becomes honest, transformed by forgiveness.

What happens when we repent and confess our sins, trusting in Christ as our Savior? God forgives us! "If we confess our sins, [God] is faithful and just and will forgive us our sins and purify us from all unrighteousness" (1 John 1:9). Isaiah's experience upon his confession was the cauterization of his sinful lips with a coal from the altar and a wonderful promise, "See, this has touched your lips; your guilt is taken away and your sin atoned for" (Isaiah 6:7). In theological terms, our confession leads to the removal of our sin.

Jesus scandalized the religious aristocracy by forgiving the sins of people. Luke tells us the story of men who carried a friend to Jesus and lowered him through the roof (Luke 5:17–26). When Jesus saw their faith, he pronounced the man forgiven. Offended, the Pharisees and teachers of the law began thinking to themselves, "Who is this fellow who speaks blasphemy? Who can forgive sins but God alone?" (Luke 5:21). Jesus answered, "'But that you may know that the Son of Man has authority on earth to forgive sins. . . .' He said to the paralyzed man, 'I tell you, get up, take your mat and go home'" (Luke 5:24). Immediately, the man was healed.

The same Lord who taught his disciples to pray "Forgive us our debts as we also have forgiven our debtors" (Matthew 6:12) forgave the very ones who crucified him. Jesus prayed from the cross, "Father, forgive them, for they do not know what they are doing" (Luke 23:34).

The story of salvation is the story of forgiveness. Paul also showed Jesus as the source of forgiveness for all who believe in him. For example, Paul defined "redemption though [Christ's] blood" as "the forgiveness of sins" (Eph. 1:7). Paul also wrote, "God made you alive with Christ. He forgave us all our sins, having canceled the written code, with its regulations, that was against us and that stood opposed to us; he took it away, nailing it to the cross" (Colossians 2:13).

Adoption: God Makes Us His Children

Have you heard the expression, *We are all God's children?* Although it sounds appealing, we do not become children of God simply by being born into this world. In that sense, we are all God's creation. We truly become children of God, though, through salvation. Although we are not born as God's children, we can be *born again* as God's children.

For as long as I can remember I have loved the love of those who adopt children. In some cases, the adoption rescues a child from danger and hopelessness. Paul explained God's adopting love, "In love, [God] predestined us to be adopted as his sons through Jesus Christ, in accordance with his pleasure and will" (Eph. 1:4–5) The same Greek word translated "adopted as his son" to describe God's work of salvation is translated "sonship" in Romans 8:15: ". . . You received the Spirit of sonship. And by him we cry 'Abba, Father.'"

We truly needed to be adopted. Before God adopted us into his family we had the "the spirit of slavery leading to fear" (Rom. 8:15, NASB). Jesus promised, "I will not leave you as orphans; I will come to you" (John 14:18).

Even we who were raised by our biological parents know the sense of being spiritually orphaned. We know how it feels, as the writer

G. K. Chesterton (1874–1936) said, to feel somehow homesick even when we are at home.[7] As created human beings, we acknowledge that God has created us all. Only through salvation, however, do we become children of God.

Some years ago when my brother and his wife took a nephew into their family because his parents had died, they raised him as their eldest son. We had the chance to watch James grow up before our eyes.

More recently, a cousin and her young daughter moved to Texas from Louisiana, fleeing Hurricane Gustav. After living with us in Houston for a week or so, my cousin and her daughter moved into the Texas Baptist Children's Home in Round Rock, Texas. There the gracious people of Children at Heart Ministries cared for them. On Christmas Eve, we received a phone call that my cousin had passed away unexpectedly. Now our family is in the process of bringing my cousin's daughter, this precious little girl, into our home. I remember walking with her in the park behind our house that first summer and her saying to me, "I want to live at your house." More recently still, she chose a *bottle cap* necklace with initials on it. Looking for her given last name, she opted instead for the letter *B*, symbolizing what will be her new last name.

We are delighted that God is granting us the privilege of loving this precious little girl in our home. How must the heavenly Father feel when we realize he wants to adopt us and we choose to go by his name as *Christians*, followers of the Christ.

Not always patiently, we are waiting for the completion of the adoption. Similarly, our own spiritual adoption is not yet complete. Salvation still awaits its culmination, "Not only so, but we ourselves, who have the firstfruits of the Spirit groan inwardly as we wait eagerly for our adoption as sons, the redemption of our bodies. For in this hope we were saved" (Rom. 8:23). Even though the work has been completed, we wait for that moment when we will be finally transformed to become God's children indeed.

Adoption is another way of describing our regeneration and justification in Christ. Tim Keller, a Presbyterian minister, helps us here, explaining

*Our adoption means we are loved like Christ is loved. We are hon-
ored like he is honored—every one of us—no matter what. Your
circumstances cannot hinder or threaten that promise. . . . Paul is not
promising you better life circumstances; he is promising you a far better
life. He's promising you a life of greatness. He is promising you a life of
joy. He's promising you a life of humility. He's promising you a life of
nobility. He's promising you a life that goes on forever.*[8]

Reconciliation: God Brings Us Close

Remember in the story of Adam and Eve's fall that their sin alienated them and their descendants from God. Their eviction from the
Garden of Eden revealed the response of a holy God to sinful choices.
We further hear the pain of this isolation in the words of David, "Do
not cast me from your presence or take your Holy Spirit from me"
(Ps. 51:11). Christ's work on the cross brought reconciliation. Paul
wrote, ". . . God was reconciling the world to himself in Christ, not
counting men's sins against them" (2 Cor. 5:18).

Why do we need to be reconciled? Our sin alienates us from God. Paul
described unbelievers' situation in sober terms, stating, "You see, at
just the right time, when we were still powerless, Christ died for the
ungodly. . . . But God demonstrates his own love for us in this: While
we were still sinners, Christ died for us. . ." (Rom. 5:6–8). In Romans
5:10, he describes us as "God's enemies." So, note that in Romans
5:6–8, 10, Paul described our plight with four words: "powerless";
"ungodly"; "sinners"; and "enemies." First, we were unable to save
ourselves, "powerless." Second, we were not righteous or good but
"ungodly." Third, as "sinners," we had *missed the mark.* Fourth, worst
of all, we were "enemies" of God. The word for "enemies" comes from
a root that means in this context *those who hated God.* An unbeliever
might take exception to such a description. Are we really that bad?
Paul answered, *Yes.* Paul wrote to the church at Colosse, "Once you
were alienated from God and were enemies in your minds because of
your evil behavior" (Col. 1:21). We have distanced ourselves from God
by our own sinful choices. This is why we need reconciliation.

Who reconciled us? God did, through Jesus Christ. Notice the collaboration. Jesus was not stepping forward to placate the anger of God. Rather, God planned to use the sacrifice of his Son to bring us to himself. "For God was pleased to have all his fullness dwell in him and through him to reconcile to himself all things, whether things on earth or things in heaven, by making peace through his blood shed on the cross" (Col.1:19–20).

How does the reconciliation take place? Our spiritual reconciliation comes specifically through the death of Christ. Paul continued in his letter to the church at Rome with a classic formulation of the concept of reconciliation through the cross.

> *For if, when we were God's enemies, we were reconciled to him through the death of his Son, how much more having been reconciled shall we be saved through his life! Not only is this so, but we also rejoice in God through our Lord Jesus Christ, through whom we have now received reconciliation (Rom. 5:10–11)*

Colossians 1:22 adds, "But now he has reconciled you by Christ's physical body through death to present you holy in his sight, without blemish and free from accusation."

What is the extent of this reconciliation? God not only intends to reconcile us to himself but also to one another. In Christ all of the barriers between humankind are broken as Christ becomes "our peace" (Eph. 2:14). He invites all *back to the table* literally in the Lord's Supper.

Luke 15:11–32 records Jesus' marvelous story of reconciliation between a lost son and his father. Responding to critics, Jesus told about a lost coin, a lost sheep, and a lost son. In each case, the subjects of the story rejoiced greatly in finding what had been lost. The story of the lost son reveals to us God's work in salvation. When the prodigal son came to himself and returned to his loving father, he received a wonderful welcome. The father had been waiting, looking for his son. When the son was still far off, the father suspended decorum and ran to his son, embracing him and giving him a robe, ring, and shoes to welcome him into a full restoration of relationship. This is reconciliation.

Legend has it that a young man named Paco ran away from his home in Spain. His father searched the streets of the city, looking for some sign of his son. When the father could not find his son, he took out an ad in the local paper saying, *Paco. Whatever you have done, wherever you have been, all is forgiven. I will meet you at the Hotel Montana in Madrid on Tuesday at noon.* The father arrived to find his son and eight hundred other young men named Paco who were longing for restoration with their fathers.[9]

Are you looking for the Father? He is looking for us, longing to save us and bring us into his new community of the redeemed.

CHAPTER *Six*

A Moment and a Lifetime

"... Being confident of this, that he who began a good work in you will carry it on to completion until the day of Christ Jesus."

—PHILIPPIANS 1:6

HOW LONG DOES IT TAKE to become a Christian? A moment. And a lifetime.

A young father was pushing a shopping cart containing a screaming baby boy through the supermarket. The father could be heard muttering gently under his breath, "Easy, Freddy, calm down now. Everything's all right, boy. Come on, Freddy, don't be upset."

A woman who was also shopping commended the father, saying, "I admire your strength. You are very patient with little Freddy."

The young father looked up glumly and said, "Lady, I am Freddy."

Most if not all of us can identify with this man's attempts to avoid making a mistake. How do we grow and become better?

Salvation begins for each person in a moment of surrender to Christ. Thus the experience of conversion, regeneration, or justification happens in a moment's time when a person answers God's call to salvation by saying, *Yes*. When we say, *I have been saved*, we generally are referring to the experience of conversion. Scripture speaks of our salvation not only as an event at a point in time but also as an ongoing process, however.

We oversimplify salvation when we say we were justified, we are being sanctified, and we will be glorified. The New Testament uses all of these terms to refer both to moments in time and to processes over time. Baptist theologian E. Y. Mullins (1860–1928) defined and explained this dual nature of sanctification, stating that sanctification is (1) "the state of one who is set apart to the service of God, who belongs to God" and (2) "the inner transformation of one thus set apart, the actual realization of holy character."[1] For our purposes, however, we will treat the ongoing process of sanctification as the development of a holy life. We often speak of this process as spiritual growth.[2]

Toward a Definition of Sanctification

In both the Old Testament and the New Testament, *to sanctify* means *to make holy* or *to set apart as distinct*. The Old Testament uses the verb *qadash*, which means *to make holy*. In context, the word speaks of anything set apart for God. So priests were holy, and certain days were considered holy, along with holy implements of worship and holy places like the temple.[3]

In the New Testament, the Greek word *hagios* similarly means *holy*. The New Testament tends to apply the word more exclusively to people instead of places, dates, and things. In fact, the early believers struggled with those who were more focused on dates and foods instead of on relationship with Christ. Paul corrected them, writing, "Therefore do not let anyone condemn you in matters of food and drink or of observing festivals, new moons, or Sabbaths. These are only a shadow of what is to come, but the substance belongs to Christ" (Colossians 2:16–17, NRSV).

A good friend invited me to fish with him for rainbow trout at Mother Neff State Park near Gatesville, Texas. Having fished for trout while growing up in Germany and Montana, I jumped at the chance. Unfortunately, the can of corn I brought as bait turned out to be cream-style corn. Imagine us trying to thread those husks of corn on the hooks.

Eventually we bought the right kind of bait and returned to fish. I hooked what looked to be the largest trout of all time, judging by the way my rod bent double. Instead of landing a trout, I reeled in a large channel catfish. Immediately, my good friend, who tended toward some rather strict views, said, "You can't eat that fish."

"Why not?" I asked honestly.

"It doesn't have scales," he exclaimed and explained from the Old Testament law (Leviticus 11:9–12).

I immediately claimed Colossians 2:16–17 and told him about our newfound freedom in Christ to eat catfish if we choose. I'm not sure he was convinced. Whatever the case, holiness is not about eating catfish or not. Paul's words ring true today, "For the kingdom of God is not a matter of eating and drinking, but of righteousness, peace and joy in the Holy Spirit" (Romans 14:17).

Sanctification creates and describes a new position and status before God. In Christ believers already possess *positional* sanctification. Nevertheless, this position has not fully translated into the lives of believers. The process that results in our transformation has been termed *conditional* sanctification. It includes making progress in our current situation in both "character and conduct."[4] We hear this in Paul's words, "It is God's will that you should be sanctified: that you should avoid sexual immorality. . . . For God did not call us to be impure, but to live a holy life" (1 Thessalonians 4:3, 7).

At another level, our sanctification will someday become complete at the Second Coming of Jesus.[5] Paul wrote, "May he strengthen your hearts so that you will be blameless and holy in the presence of our God and Father when our Lord Jesus comes with all his holy ones" (1 Thess. 3:13). So sanctification is a gift already given, a growth that is occurring, and a goal we will attain.[6]

The Possibility of Sanctification

How do we stop sinning? Some have tried to use legal means. The prohibition movement in the early twentieth century in the United States sought to make drinking illegal. Most agree now that this experiment failed. Recently, cursing was prohibited for a week in Los Angeles, California. Two years earlier, upset by the way his friends in seventh grade cursed and told dirty jokes, McKay Hatch set up the No Cussing Club. The club now has members from all over the world. The example of this fourteen-year-old boy inspired Los Angeles County Supervisor Michael Antonovich to instate the Cuss-Free Week in the city. Antonovich hopes that positive peer pressure will prevail through this emphasis.[7]

Can sin just be outlawed? If only it were that easy! Old Testament law forbade sin, but as Paul noted in Galatians, the law did not save (Galatians 3:10–11). God is interested not only in eliminating sin from our lives but also in creating holiness in them. The idea of becoming holy is rooted in the Old Testament. When Isaiah saw God in the temple, he heard the resounding echo of angels' voices shouting, "Holy, Holy, Holy is the Lord Almighty" (Isaiah 6:1). Immediately, the prophet recognized his own sinfulness. Taking a coal from the altar, an angel cleansed Isaiah of guilt and sin. Having been cleansed, Isaiah heard God's missional call and answered, "Here I am. Send me!" (Isa. 6:8).

Is such cleansing possible for us? Can we really be free not only from the penalty of sin but also from the power of sin? In a familiar passage, Paul described the struggle for holiness, "I do not understand what I do. For what I want to do I do not do, but what I hate I do" (Rom. 7:15). He continued, "For what I do is not the good I want to do; no, the evil I do not want to do—this I keep on doing" (Rom. 7:19). Many believers resonate with these passages, as though this is the normative, normal Christian life. But Paul continued, "What a wretched man I am! Who will rescue me from this body of death? Thanks be to God—through Jesus Christ our Lord!" (Rom. 7:24–25). We must not stop even with these words because Paul continued,

"Therefore there is now no condemnation for those who are in Christ Jesus" (Rom. 8:1).

So, in Christ, believers find freedom from the penalty of our sins, and more. God accomplished our sanctification in Christ as well, "in order that the righteous requirements of the law might be fully met in us, who do not live according to the sinful nature but according to the Spirit" (Rom.8:4). While it is true that "the sinful mind is hostile to God" and "those controlled by the sinful nature cannot please God," (Rom.8:7–8), Paul believed better things about followers of Christ. "You, however, are controlled not by the sinful nature but by the Spirit, if the Spirit of God lives in you" (Rom. 8:9).

Can we become holy without becoming *holier than thou?* Those who are growing in holiness do not put others off with a smug sense of spiritual self-satisfaction. A familiar saying states, "You can be so heavenly minded that you are no earthly good." Having never seen that idea in the Scriptures, I am convinced that there is little danger of it actually occurring. In fact the Apostle Paul urged the Colossians, "Since, then, you have been raised with Christ, set your hearts on things above, where Christ is seated at the right hand of God. Set your minds on things above, not on earthly things" (Col. 3:1–2). C. S. Lewis (1898–1963) wrote, "If you read history you will find that the Christians who did most for the present world were precisely those who thought most of the next. It is since Christians have largely ceased to think of the other world that they have become so ineffective in this one."[8] It would seem that the greater danger for us is not that we become so heavenly minded that we are no earthly good. May God instead protect us from being so earthly minded that we are no heavenly good!

The Purpose of Sanctification

Not only is God holy, but God intends to make *us* holy also. "You are to be holy to me because I, the LORD, am holy and I have set you apart from the nations to be my own" (Lev. 20:26). From the beginning the word "holy" described objects set apart for God alone. So the temple, its furniture, and the priests who offered sacrifices were to consecrate themselves or set themselves apart for God's purposes alone. We may feel the same way about the places we worship God. Most of us would be unwilling to play a football game in the worship centers of our churches. Somehow it feels that this space should be reserved for worship alone. The Scriptures teach us, "The earth is the LORD's and everything in it, the world, and all who live in it. . . . Who may ascend the hill of the LORD? Who may stand in his holy place? He who has clean hands and a pure heart, who does not lift up his soul to an idol or swear by what is false" (Psalm 24:1–4).

The New Testament extends this idea to include not only a select group of spiritual leaders but all who are followers of Christ. In the Sermon on the Mount, Jesus said to his disciples, "Be perfect, therefore, as your heavenly Father is perfect" (Matthew 5:48). The word "perfect" in this context means *complete* or *fulfilling the desired purpose.* In sanctification, God moves his people closer to the ideal established at creation when humankind walked with God sinlessly in the garden.

Paul used the image of becoming like Jesus. He spoke of being "crucified with Christ" (Gal. 2:20). He wrote what has become a favorite verse for many,

> *And we know that in all things God works for the good of those who love him, who have been called according to his purpose. For those God foreknew he also predestined to be conformed to the likeness of his Son that he might be the firstborn among many brothers (Rom. 8:28–29).*

What was Paul saying? We might begin with what Paul clearly did not mean. Paul did not mean that everything that happens to everybody is good, or that everything will work out. Instead, he was telling us that God himself is working—literally *synergizing all things together for good.* God takes the good and the bad events in our lives and shapes them together to create ultimate good.

What is that good? Does it mean everything will go believers' way and that we will always feel good? Will traffic part like the Red Sea before us? Will our sports teams always win? Will we become instantly healthy, wealthy, and wise? No. The good that God is working toward is the process of conforming us to the image of God's Son, Jesus. We were created in the image of God. Sin has marred that image. In Christ, God is restoring us to the image of his Son. God is out to make something out of us. Paul further described it as our "attaining to the whole measure of the fullness of Christ" (Eph. 4:13).

The Barriers to Sanctification

Why is it so hard to live a holy life? We face both internal and external obstacles to spiritual growth.[9] Internally, we fight against "the flesh," as Paul termed it (see Gal. 5:16, NRSV, NASB). Flesh is our predisposition toward sin, apart from the control of the Spirit. As Christians, this part of our human nature has been crucified, but we must still die daily. We must be careful not to coddle or feed this part of our nature. Strongholds of sinfulness develop in our lives through undisciplined habits. Like the sheep that goes astray, we can nibble our way into trouble. Someone has said, "Sin always takes us farther than we want to go, keeps us longer than we want to stay, and costs more than we want to pay."

Externally, the world we live in is quite congenial to the unholy life. John used the word "world" (*kosmos*) as a synonym for all that is evil (1 John 2:15–17). For this reason, he admonished believers not to love the world or the things of the world. Behind this opposition stand the spiritual forces of evil in high places (Eph.6:12). But the external opposition to spiritual growth from the world around us need not win the day. "The one who is in you is greater than the one who is in the world" (1 John 4:4). Through faith we overcome the world and its opposition (1 John 5:4–5).

How? First, we must place our trust in Jesus' victory over sin. "For we do not have a high priest who is unable to sympathize with our weaknesses, but we have one who has been tempted in every way, just as we are—yet was without sin. Let us then approach the throne of grace with confidence" (Hebrews 5:15).

Related to this truth is that we should remember God's kindness. How quickly we forget God's kindness. Adam and Eve were willing to throw away all the goodness of God for one piece of fruit. They doubted God's goodness to them. What if they had called out to God instead of believing the serpent? After all God had done for them, could not they have trusted him? God's compassion especially invites us to trust him.

We need supernatural help to overcome sin because spiritual forces work to tempt and destroy us (Eph. 2:2; 6:12). The good news is that when Christians experience temptation God makes his power available to us. Paul wrote, "No temptation has seized you except what is common to man. And God is faithful; he will not let you be tempted beyond what you can bear. But when you are tempted, he will also provide a way out so that you can stand up under it" (1 Cor. 10:13). It remains for Christians to avail themselves of God's great power.

Second, we should avoid temptation. One senior pastor warned his handsome new associate about the dangers of immorality in the ministry. The assistant said that he always did his socializing in a group setting and concluded, "There is safety in numbers." The wise senior pastor agreed, "Yes that is true, but there is more safety in Exodus."

When faced with temptation, we should run like Joseph running from Potiphar's wife when she invited him to betray her husband with her and commit adultery (Genesis 39). In the New Testament, Paul instructed, "Flee from sexual immorality" (1 Cor. 6:18). For the word "flee," Paul used the Greek word *feugo*, which is the source of the English word *fugitive*. Either we become *fugitives* from sin or *fugitives* from God.

Third, we should actively fight against sin in our lives. James taught, "Resist the devil, and he will flee from you" (James 4:7). We should "make no provision for the flesh in regard to its lusts" (Rom. 13:14, NASB). Hebrews states, "In your struggle against sin, you have not yet resisted to the point of shedding your blood" (Heb. 12:4). Paul testified of his own efforts, writing, "Therefore I do not run like a man running aimlessly. I do not fight like a man beating the air. No, I beat my body and make it my slave so that after I have preached to others, I myself will not be disqualified for the prize" (1 Cor. 9:26–27). The evangelist Billy Sunday (1862–1935) expressed this idea in his colorful way, "I'm against sin. I'll kick it as long as I've got a foot, and

I'll fight it as long as I've got a fist. I'll butt it as long as I've got a head. I'll bite it as long as I've got a tooth. When I'm old and fistless and footless and toothless, I'll gum it till I go home to glory and it goes home to perdition."

The Process of Sanctification

The story is told that Michelangelo (1475–1564), the great sculptor and painter, was pushing a heavy rock up a small incline to his work area so he could make a sculpture. A neighbor watched him as he worked to get the rock in place. Finally he asked, "Why do you labor so hard over that ugly, heavy piece of rock?" Michelangelo said, "Because there is an angel inside that wants to come out." The Divine Artist works in our lives, because he not only sees who we are but also sees who we can be!

Only the triune God can make God's people holy. "May God himself, the God of peace, sanctify you through and through" (1 Thess. 5:23). In 1 Corinthians, Paul added, "It is because of [God] that you are in Christ Jesus, who has become for us wisdom from God—that is, our righteousness, holiness and redemption" (1 Cor. 1:30). Because God works for our sanctification, we place our faith or trust in him to make us into the people we could never be on our own. So the faith that leads to justification continues in the process of being saved or what we call sanctification.

Pastor and author John Ortberg has compared the experience of sanctification or spiritual transformation to crossing an ocean. Some try to be good on their own in a way that resembles taking a rowboat across the ocean. Others disavow all effort and rely on God's grace. They drift along on a raft. But neither of these methods is fruitful. A better analogy is the sailboat. Only God can make the wind blow, but we must set our sails to catch the breezes. Our God chooses to cooperate with believers. In this sense, the work of sanctification is both God's work and ours.[10]

So, first, sanctification is God's work in believers. "For it is by grace that you have been saved, through faith—and this not from yourselves, it is the gift of God—not by works so that no one can boast. For we are God's workmanship, created in Christ Jesus to do good works which God prepared in advance for us to do" (Eph. 2:8–10). Clearly believers are saved only by God's grace. God gives us the ability to believe, so that we cannot even assume credit for our faith. Salvation remains God's gift, leaving us no room to boast. Paul reached the crescendo when he called us "God's workmanship," or God's *poem* or God's *masterpiece*. But this master-work calls forth our works.

Second, sanctification is our response to God's work in our lives. Followers of Christ are not saved by works, but we are saved *unto* works (Eph. 2:10). For this reason, holiness or sanctification can refer to moral qualities God develops and we implement in our behavior. Sanctification rests in part on the believer's obedience to Christ. "But now that you have been set free from sin and have become slaves to God, the benefit you reap leads to holiness and the result is eternal life" (Rom. 6:22). We are to "make every effort to live in peace with all men and to be holy; without holiness no one will see the Lord" (Heb. 12:14).

An old hymn we sang at my first pastorate in Pleasant Grove, Falls County, Texas, reminds us that holiness involves time. I can still hear the voices almost plaintively plead, "Take time to be holy. . . ."[11] It is hard to be holy in a hurry. Maybe the great surprise should be how much we resemble our Lord in view of how little time we spend in prayer. My friend Dr. Howard Batson, pastor of First Baptist Church of Amarillo, Texas, once told me of the painstaking work of an artist who set out to restore the beauty of the artwork in their church's sanctuary. The artist glued chips of paint down carefully and meticulously to bring the artwork back to life. Sanctification requires no less attention to the spiritual details of our lives. It is a painstaking but worthwhile process. We can be thankful we are not in it alone.

In his Letter to the Philippians, Paul amplified this dual responsibility for sanctification. He focused first on the human element and next on God's work. He instructed, ". . . Work out your salvation with fear and trembling, for it is God who works in you to will and to act according to his good purpose" (Phil. 2:12–13). Paul did not instruct them to work *for* their salvation. Such an instruction would contradict so much of what Paul wrote on the subject of grace and works. But following Christ requires a conscious transformation with believers' full cooperation. God, who has done so much for us, deserves our full commitment to the process of sanctification. Reverence for God provides our motivation for sanctification.

Paul further explained that we are not in the work of sanctification alone. "For it is God who works in you to will and to act according to his good purpose" (Phil. 2:13). Paul offered good news for us as we work out our salvation: God is working. This work is both personal and corporate—"in you" is plural. Too, God is working both in intentions and actions—"to will and to act." This very fact calls us to deep communion with the Father.

Some years ago, on a Friday morning, I was frantically preparing to preach, parsing every word, speaking each sentence out loud. As I worked, I sensed that God had something to say to me about my meticulous routine for preparation. I was so concerned about *doing* the right thing. It was as if God said to me, *You would be happy if you preached well this weekend, whether or not you had communed with me. But if you will commune with me, I will give you the words to speak on my behalf.* This realization liberated me both in my living for Christ and in my preaching. Naturally, we would be content to *do,* but God prefers that we *be* with him. Being precedes doing, every time. Who we are will inevitably emerge in what we do.

Philippians 2:13 reminds us, further, that God is working for a reason—"according to his good purpose." Once again we see that God's design for our lives as believers is good. In the work of sanctifying us, making us like Christ, God does the heavy lifting and invites us to join in the work. One can hardly become like Christ if one is unwilling to participate in the process.

The Power for Sanctification

Not long ago a friend attempted to justify sin by saying, "I should not condemn what I do, because then I would be hating the way that God made me and that would be wrong." Of course, God did not create us so that we might sin. We can never blame God for our choices. God wants to help us overcome sin. What resources has God made available to assist us toward sanctification?

The Gospel of John gives us a front row seat to hear Jesus' prayer on the night before his crucifixion: "Sanctify them by the truth; your word is truth" (John 17:17). Jesus had given his disciples the words the Father gave him, and they had accepted his words. Now Jesus prayed that these truthful words would set his disciples apart for holiness.

To this day, believers are sanctified through the hearing and doing of the words that are preached in times of worship. In this way worship assists us toward sanctification. Our contemplation of the holiness of God not only reveals our sinfulness but creates in us a desire to grow closer to God and God's righteous ideal for our lives.

We hear a similar echo of God's work of sanctification in Paul's admonition to the Ephesian believers about marriage. "Husbands, love your wives, just as Christ loved the church and gave himself up for her to make her holy, cleansing her by the washing with water through the word" (Eph. 5:26). The words God speaks to us through Scripture serve to strengthen our sanctification. Even in these words, we hear the corporate dimension of sanctification. Truly, Christ is making each of us holy, but Christ is accomplishing this in the community of the church. Discipleship and sanctification occur primarily in community. We grow spiritually by living in intimate fellowship with God and with one another. Corporate worship is of particular benefit because of the fellowship we share with other believers. Fellowship offers both velvet and steel. On the one hand, fellow believers provide us acceptance—velvet—and on the other hand, they hold us accountable—steel.

The power for sanctification is spiritual power, mediated by the Holy Spirit. Resurrection power ensures our sanctification. Paul told the church that the same power that raised Christ from the dead would empower them to overcome temptation (Rom. 8:11; 1 Cor. 6:14). As believers, we "live by the Spirit," we are "led by the Spirit," and we "keep in step with the Spirit" (Gal. 5:16–26). When we live by the Spirit, we "will not gratify the desires of the sinful nature" (Gal. 5:16). As my seminary professor Jack Gray used to say, "When we are bumped we spill whatever has filled us." When we are "led by the Spirit," we are not bound by the law and legalism (Gal. 5:18). God the Holy Spirit produces fruit in our lives (Gal. 5:22–23). Since this Spirit has given us life, we are not to lag behind, but we are to desire to "keep in step with the Spirit" (Gal. 5:25).

The Proof of Our Sanctification

Are we there yet? Our kids have always asked this question as we travel. When we answer, *Not yet*, they ask, *How much longer?*

We might ask the same questions about sanctification. How can we tell whether we are progressing in sanctification? If perfection is the goal of our sanctification, how do we know whether we have arrived? In Paul's day, some just gave up trying (see Rom. 6:1). Their convoluted rationale sounds familiar in our day: *God loves to forgive, and I love to sin. So the more I sin, the more grace God gives. So I should continue to sin.* Paul answered with a strong prohibition, "By no means!" (Rom. 6:2).

On the other hand, through the years, many have claimed to overcome sin completely. Where do the *perfectionists* find their footing in Scripture? Some appeal to 1 John 3:6, "No one who lives in him keeps on sinning. No one who continues to sin has either seen him or known him." John also wrote, "If we claim to be without sin, we deceive ourselves and the truth is not in us" (1 John 1:8). Some mean by sinless perfection that they no longer sin deliberately or consciously. Others reduce the idea to good intentions. Theologian W. T. Conner was right, "Almost anyone could reach a standard of perfection if you would let him bring the standard of perfection down low enough."[12] Even the Apostle Paul did not believe he had attained perfection yet but continued to stretch to lay hold of God's purpose for his life (Phil. 3:12–14).

God sets the standard for holiness, because God embodies and defines it. As we contemplate the absolute holiness of God, we must conclude with Isaiah that we are unclean and everybody we know is unclean (Isa. 6:3–5). We also hear it in the words of the Apostle Paul as he admitted to being "the worst" of sinners (1 Tim.1:15).

The moment we claim to have overcome all sin in our lives, we find ourselves guilty of the sin of pride. Christ has not called us to be *holier than thou*. Rather Christ has called us to be *holy*.

As we grow we must not become self-satisfied or complacent. The Christian life calls us upward and onward as we become conformed progressively to the image of Christ. In funeral services, as I contemplate the lives of some of the great saints with whom I have been privileged to serve, I sometimes say, "We may wonder why she was so kind and good. The answer is clear. She was the way she was because our God is the way he is. She was becoming more like Christ. She had progressed in her sanctification to the point that we saw Christ clearly formed in her life."

A businessman decided to landscape his grounds. He employed a person with a doctorate in horticulture. This person was extremely knowledgeable. Because the businessman was very busy and traveled a lot, he kept emphasizing to the person the need to develop the garden in a way that would require little or no maintenance on his part. He insisted on automatic sprinklers and other labor-saving devices. Finally the employee stopped the businessman and challenged, "There's one thing you need to deal with before we go any further. If there's no gardener, there's no garden!"

Just so, there is no shortcut to sanctification. Growing to spiritual maturity requires time, commitment, and effort.

Jesus said, "Blessed are those who hunger and thirst for righteousness, for they will be filled" (Matt.5:6). God will honor the desires of our hearts. Let us resolve with the theologian Søren Kierkegaard (1813–1855), "Now, with God's help, I shall become myself."[13]

CHAPTER *Seven*

Saved into a Community

"For we were all baptized by one Spirit into one body—whether Jews or Greeks, slave or free—and we were all given the one Spirit to drink. . . . Now you are the body of Christ, and each one of you is a part of it."

—1 CORINTHIANS 12:13, 27

IN HER BOOK *Traveling Mercies*, Anne Lamott shares a story her minister told that illustrates well the necessary presence of others in our journey of faith. She said that when the minister was a child, the minister's best friend got lost.

She was very frightened. Finally a policeman stopped to help her. He put her in the passenger seat of his car, and they drove around until she finally saw her church. She pointed it out to the policeman, and then she told him firmly, "You could let me out now. This is my church, and I can always find my way home from here."

Lamott further writes of herself: "And that is why I have stayed so close to [my church]—because no matter how bad I am feeling, how lost or lonely or frightened, when I see the faces of the people at my church . . . I can always find my way home."[1]

The ideas about salvation with which we are familiar might lead some to believe salvation is a solo flight. Indeed, each person must choose Christ in order to be saved. However, salvation also provides an entry point into a community called the church. In fact, were it not for the Christian community, most of us would not have come to Christ in the first place.

The Community of Believers

"You cannot have God as your Father unless you have the church for your Mother." So wrote Cyprian of Carthage in the third century A.D.[2] Is the church essential to salvation? Each individual must believe in Christ to become a Christian, of course. Baptists have long taught *soul competency*, the idea that each individual is capable of receiving Christ without the mediation of any ecclesiastical or priestly authority. Without diminishing this Baptist distinctive, we must recognize that disciples are developed in community. We can become Christians without the mediation of the church, but we grow as Christians in fellowship with other believers. Jesus showed us the way by calling out the Twelve and investing his life and love in them. The church at its best assimilates and incorporates new believers.

When 3,000 became followers of Christ at Pentecost, the church immediately created community for them (see Acts 2:42–47). At two churches I have served, we have used the acronym *WISE* to describe life in the community of those whom God has saved. The four letters invite us to consider four identity markers of the church: *W*orship; *I*nstruction; *S*haring; and *E*vangelism.

The Saved Community at Worship

The new believers devoted themselves to the worship of God (Acts 2:42). The word for "devoted" is *proskartereo*, which means *to continue steadfastly.* Worship begins with undivided devotion to God. In fact, whatever we devote ourselves to becomes our object of worship. At many musical events and sporting events, the response of the fans looks more like worship than recreation.

How often did these early believers worship? Luke tells us, "Every day they continued to meet together in the temple courts" (Acts 2:46). We who have experienced salvation are to live lives of worship. The writer of Hebrews admonished, "Let us not give up meeting together as some are in the habit of doing, but let us encourage one another—and all the more as you see the Day approaching" (Heb. 10:25).

Where did the early church worship? Not only did the early believers meet at the temple but also in homes (Acts 2:46). Believers practice worship wherever they are, in various settings. This practice opposes the compartmentalization of life so common in our culture. All too often, the church is viewed as a building and location or a place to go. At our church, I never greet worshipers with the words, "Welcome to worship *at* Tallowood," but rather "Welcome to worship *with* Tallowood." The church is composed of people; it's not a place.

How should we worship? We follow the devotion of the early believers who manifested worship in both attitudes and actions.

Attitudes in Worship

What attitudes do we see in this early church? "Everyone was filled with awe. . ." (Acts 2:43). "Awe" characterized the worship of the early church. They worshiped with a deep sense of reverence and anticipation for what God might do among them. Wonders and signs took place as the people trusted in God.

Could it be that in our efforts to identify with and relate to our culture, the church has lost its sense of awe? Looking at the story of the healing of the lame man (Acts 3:6–8), one church leader reportedly said about his opulent church, "The church no longer has to say, 'Silver or gold I do not have.'" His companion answered, "Neither do we say any longer, 'In the name of Jesus Christ of Nazareth, walk.'" Where is the holy hush among the people of God? Where is the sense of anticipation? Do we come to worship with any expectation that God might do something great among us?

The early church also worshiped with gladness. These early believers coupled their awe with adoration. We find it in the words "praising God" (Acts 2:47). What if we were caught in adoration? The British church leader and theologian William Temple (1881–1944) once defined worship as

> the submission of all of our nature to God. It is the quickening of conscience by His holiness, nourishment of mind by His truth, purifying of imagination by His beauty, opening of the heart to His love, and submission of will to His purpose. And all this gathered up in adoration is the greatest of human expressions of which we are capable.[3]

Does joy characterize our worship? Joy is the mark of Christian worship. When believers are caught in adoration, there is a greater chance that unbelievers will want to come and share in the joy. Paul envisioned an unbeliever coming in and being "convinced by all that he is a sinner" when the "secrets of his heart will be laid bare. So he will fall down and worship God exclaiming, 'God is really among you!'" (1 Corinthians 14:24–25).

Further, these early believers worshiped sincerely. They did not pretend to live one way while in fact they lived another. Christian worship must be sincere and authentic to impact a non-Christian culture.

Only when we worship do we fulfill God's ultimate purpose for our lives. "The first business then of a church is not evangelism, nor missions, nor benevolence; it is worship. The worship of God in Christ should be at the center of all else that the church does. It is the mainspring of all the activity of the church."[4]

Actions in Worship

What did the believers do in worship? They demonstrated devotion in teaching, fellowship, the breaking of bread, and prayer. We shall look at teaching and fellowship more closely in the next two sections and the next chapter. Important for our purposes in this chapter is the obedience expressed in worship. By eating the Lord's Supper and praying, the disciples were consciously choosing to obey Christ. With so many voices speaking about the meaning of worship, we should not miss their exemplary obedience.

The expression "breaking of bread" likely refers to their practice of the Lord's Supper (Acts 2:42). We also read that they "broke bread" from house to house, but this seems to refer to spending time and eating daily meals together (Acts 2:46). Jesus established the Lord's Supper as an ordinance for his disciples to obey. The Gospel of John tells us that Jesus first washed the disciples' feet as a reminder of their need to follow his example of servanthood (John 13:1–17). At the Passover Jesus broke bread and said, "This is my body given for you; do this in remembrance of me" (Luke 22:19). Afterward Jesus took the cup and said, "This cup is the new covenant in my blood, which is poured out for you" (Luke 22:20). The Gospel of Matthew adds that Jesus' blood offers the forgiveness of sins (Matt. 26:28).

In 1 Corinthians, we find perhaps the earliest New Testament writing on the subject of the Lord's Supper.[5] The Christians in Corinth were struggling in their meetings, doing "more harm than good" (1 Corinthians 11:17). Their lack of unity nullified the community effect of the Lord's Supper. Astonishingly, they took the reenactment of the unselfish act of Christ's crucifixion and made it a selfish event in which they ate without waiting for one another, leaving nothing for the latecomers. In contrast to Christ's voluntary humiliation of himself, they humiliated others by leaving out the poor (1 Cor. 11:22). Paul passed on the truth about the Lord's Supper that he himself had received. The Lord's Supper is a time for holy reflection and commemoration. Jesus said about both the bread and the cup, do this "in remembrance of me" (1 Cor.11: 25). Many in our world drink alcohol to *forget* their troubles, but the church drinks at the Lord's table to *remember* what Christ has done for us. Far from clouding our thoughts, the bread and the cup clarify our understanding of Christ's sacrifice for us.

The Lord's Supper is also a time of holy proclamation. When we eat and drink, we "proclaim the Lord's death. . ." (1 Cor. 11:26). At the table, the whole church preaches. We proclaim our faith in the Lord who died for us. Our celebration reenacts the crucifixion and tells the story again so nobody can forget what Jesus has done for us. In the Lord's Supper we lift our eyes in holy anticipation "until he comes" (1 Cor. 11:26). Too, by eating together, we affirm our confidence that Christ will return. We eat in anticipation of the great wedding feast of the Lamb (Revelation 19:9). Some in the church at Corinth came with the wrong attitudes, not offering repentance or asking forgiveness before they ate. For this reason, Paul instructed that the Lord's Supper become a time of holy examination of their lives before believers eat and drink (1 Cor.11:28–29).

The believers also devoted themselves "to prayer" (Acts 2:42). These believers had learned the lessons of Gethsemane. Jesus had not been able to find anyone who would continue in prayer with him the night before his crucifixion (Matt. 26:40–46). But here we see the disciples had learned their lesson. When they asked Jesus to teach them to pray, Jesus taught them what we commonly call the *Lord's Prayer* (Luke 11:1–4). Then on the night before his crucifixion, Jesus prayed in their presence what might more accurately be called the *Lord's Prayer* or Jesus' *High Priestly Prayer* (John 17).

After Jesus departed and invited his disciples to wait in Jerusalem, we find these believers doing nothing apart from prayer. "They all joined together constantly in prayer" (Acts 1:14). When they needed to call out a new leader to take Judas Iscariot's place, they prayed and asked God to show the one whom he had chosen (Acts 1:24). Threatened by the authorities for preaching the name of Jesus, they prayed (Acts 4:23–31). The same apostles who could not stay awake in Gethsemane told the whole church that they would give their attention to "prayer and the ministry of the word," in that order (Acts 6:4). Prayer was their first work. Our love for preaching and teaching the Bible must not precede our devotion to God in prayer.

Prayer was more of a force than a form for them. Leo Tolstoy tells the story of three hermits who lived on an island. Devoted to God, they prayed in this simple way: "Three are ye, three are we, have mercy upon us." Miracles sometimes happened when they prayed this way.

The bishop heard about the three hermits and decided they needed guidance in proper prayer. So he went to their small island. When he talked with the hermits, he realized how much they needed to learn. So one thing he did was to instruct them in the proper way to pray. In their humility, they were receptive and tried to learn.

Satisfied with his efforts, the bishop set sail back for the mainland. He was pleased with himself, having brought enlightenment to such simple, unlearned men.

That night he could not sleep and was looking across the water. Suddenly off the stern of the ship he saw something that seemed like light skimming across the ocean. It got closer and closer until he could see it was the three hermits running on top of the water, "all gleaming white, their grey beards shining, and approaching the ship. . . ."

As the bishop, the other passengers, and the crew looked on in amazement, the hermits said, "We have forgotten your teaching, servant of God. As long as we kept repeating it we remembered, but when we stopped saying it for a time, a word dropped out, and now it has all gone to pieces. We can remember nothing of it. Teach us again."

The bishop could only reply, "Your own prayer will reach the Lord, men of God. It is not for me to teach you. Pray for us sinners."[6]

The Saved Community in Instruction

In the Great Commission (Matt. 28:18–20), Jesus told his disciples to "make disciples of all nations baptizing . . . and teaching them to obey everything I have commanded you." The church at Jerusalem was committed to both parts of this commission. Today, baptismal counts often are considered the sole measure of the effectiveness of the church. Healthy churches do multiply by leading others to Christ, but they must not stop there. Churches who baptize many but never disciple the new followers of Christ are only partly fulfilling Jesus' commission. Teaching all things that Jesus commanded requires diligence and intentionality.

The new believers "devoted themselves to the apostles' teaching" (Acts 2:42). Baptist professor and author Dallas Willard has rightly decried the reality of a church filled with undiscipled disciples.[7] Let us devote ourselves to emphasize discipling those who would follow Christ, including learning the words of Scripture.

The Book of Acts tells about the exemplary congregation at Berea (Acts 17:10–15). Paul and Silas left Thessalonica and arrived in Berea to discover that the Bereans were of more noble character than the Thessalonians (who had run Paul out of town). Notice the characteristics of these noble women and men.

First, "they received the message with great eagerness" (Acts 17:11). Hungry for the truth, they waited with anticipation for a word from God.

Second, the Bereans "examined the Scriptures every day to see if what Paul said was true" (Acts 17:11). Thus, the authority of the teaching did not rest in the charisma and talent of the newest teacher in town. Instead, they went to the Scriptures to test Paul's words for truth.

Third, many "believed" the message. A congregation of Jews and prominent Greek women and men came together around the truth. Culturally, historically, and spiritually these Jews and Greeks possessed little in common with each other. But in Christ they became a church.

Fourth, they put their fledgling faith into action, protecting Paul from the Thessalonians and escorting him safely to Athens. Silas and Timothy remained to continue the discipleship process for a short season. Why is there no letter to the Bereans in our New Testament? Paul often wrote to address issues in the church. Perhaps the Bereans had no such need of correction and instruction because they grew to maturity in Christ by feeding themselves from God's word. Will this be the legacy of your church and mine?

When we have learned to digest spiritual truth, we will no longer chase every wind of doctrine that comes our way. The salvation process entails constant learning and growth through reading and practice of the teachings recorded in the Scriptures. To this day, the Bible study hour remains the best hour in the church for spiritual growth to take place. As a pastor, I consider it important to devote myself to teaching so that our people will devote themselves to learning and growing. God will surely honor these commitments.

The Saved Community Sharing Life

Newly saved believers began to share their lives together in fellowship (Acts 2:42). The word *koinonia*, translated as "fellowship," means *to share all things in common.* In Anne Ortlund's classic analogy, the early believers were more like a bag of grapes than a bag of marbles. Marbles may contact one another, but the only change they can make if shaken together is damaging. Grapes put under pressure come together to form a beautiful liquid and wonderful fragrance.[8] Christian fellowship involves more than mere sitting beside one another for one hour a week. To experience the Christian life, we must share our lives together.

Acts explains further, "All the believers were together and had everything in common" (Acts 2:44). We notice the inclusiveness of the new community: "All the believers. . . ." They originated from several different locales around the world, but in Christ they were becoming one (Acts 2:9–11).

We must always guard ourselves against *koinonia*—fellowship— becoming *koinonitis*—an *in* group with an inward focus. When believers in a local church become inwardly focused, we may lose sight of the stranger in our gates. As one unknown poet put it, our attitude becomes

> You, me, Fred, and Eleanor
> We four
> No more
> Shut the door.

The church at Jerusalem included others and shared their lives. In their commitment to unity, the believers shared all things "in common" (Acts 2:44). They sold their possessions and gave to those in need. Barnabas provided the most notable example by selling a piece of land and laying the proceeds at the feet of the apostles (Acts 4:36–37).

Some years ago a revival of giving began at New Hope First Baptist Church in Cedar Park, Texas, when a young girl gave a very special offering to the church. One Monday morning I received a green envelope with my name on it. Ushers had found it in the offering plate. I could tell from the handwriting that a child had written it. As I opened the envelope, a note fell out of the card inside. It read,

> *Dear Pastor Brooks, The Lord told me to give my savings to the church. It is quite a bit of money, but I want the church to have it. I am not a member yet, but I wanted you to know that I have just received Christ and I want to join the church soon. Sincerely, Ashley Young, a twelve year old.*

I opened the envelope expecting to find pennies and nickels. Instead, I discovered a one hundred dollar bill, two twenties, a five, some ones, and some change. I went into my secretary's office and said, "Who is Ashley Young?" She checked the records and couldn't find any record of her. I told our financial people, "Hold on to the money, don't spend it because in the near future somebody may be calling about this."

As I expected, a few weeks later, there was a guest card in the plate. Ashley's parents filled it out and said, "We'd like a visit from the pastor."

I thought, *I'll bet they do.* Not knowing whether she had informed her parents, I went that night carrying the envelope. I told them the story, and said, "Ashley, here is the money. If you want to tithe from it, or if you want to keep it. I brought it back."

After an awkward silence that lasted forever, her parents asked, "Why did you bring the money back?"

I said, "Well, I didn't know what you wanted us to do with it, or if you knew about it."

They said, "Well, you read the note. Ashley said that God had told her to give the money. We have raised her to obey God. So why did you bring it back?"

I said, "I don't know!"

But the next week after I told that story, the church followed Ashley's example and brought their savings. In one week the church gave over seven times the budget needed for a week at that time. We took the extra money and bought a home to house one homeless family at a time. The first family to move in to the house had been living in their car. This mother and teen-aged daughter became followers of Christ. Ashley's obedience led to a revival.

Not only did all the new believers share, but they shared everything they had. Acts describes this fellowship like this: "They broke bread in their homes and ate together with glad and sincere hearts" (Acts 2:46).

The table remains a place of hospitality in our world. One pastor said, "The first question a Christian should ask a guest is, 'Will you join us for lunch?'" At Tallowood we share in a meal called "Lunch with the Pastors." Our guests come and sit at table with us after a service of worship. The army of volunteers who comprise our kitchen committee serves our guests a delightful meal under the watchful eye of our "Minister of Hospitality," Barbara Justman.

Some of the sweetest memories of my childhood revolve around church meals together. In the eight or nine different churches my family attended as I grew up, potluck meals were a staple. My favorite memory is of a picnic we shared at Rhein Valley Baptist Church in Waldorf, West Germany. Military families composed of officers and enlisted people gathered in this one church. In our community, military rank could have threatened the sweetness of the church's fellowship. However, at this picnic embedded in my memory, officer and enlisted, wealthy and poor, came to the picnic and played softball and horseshoes together. But when the meal time came, we retreated to our separate tables. Some brought peanut butter and jelly sandwiches while others grilled T-bone steaks.

A new pastor, Jim Hallcom, came to the church and his first picnic with a different idea. While we played the softball game, he and others aligned all the picnic tables in rows. All the food was placed on the tables, and we shared. Some who brought sandwiches tasted steak and vice versa.

That was New Testament community. Paul wrote to the church at Galatia, "You are all sons of God through faith in Christ Jesus, for all of you who were baptized into Christ have clothed yourselves with Christ. There is neither Jew nor Greek, slave nor free, male nor female, for you are all one in Christ Jesus" (Galatians 3:26–28).

The Saved Community in Evangelism

Worship is not primarily about evangelism, but neither is it oblivious to evangelism. As these early believers shared their lives and praised God, they enjoyed the favor of all the people. Early believers were winsome in their practice of Christianity. While they worshiped, taught, and shared, God "added to their number daily those who were being saved" (Acts 2:47).

These early believers did not delegate their evangelism to the specially gifted. All were involved in the community, and all shared the story of Jesus.

As they did, the Lord added to their number. Again, we see that salvation comes at God's initiative. We are not in the work of evangelism alone. God is working through us. Those who were saved were added immediately to community. Salvation does not happen in isolation. Discipleship, if it happens at all, happens in community.

When I was in school, my wife and I lived in married student housing. The walls of the apartment complex were thin. How thin were they? They were so thin that my father-in-law accidentally drilled through the double sheetrock to hang a mirror only to find that his drill had gone into the other apartment.

For a time an international student who was single lived next to us. We were cordial at first, but soon the lifestyle choices of the single student next door created tension for us. He was lascivious and licentious, bringing women to the apartment. This annoyed me greatly.

To make matters worse, he stole my newspaper. When the delivery person threw the newspaper up over the railing, the student sneaked out and stole my newspaper. I confronted him, but he denied it. Still worse, he played awful music that offended us greatly.

Then one night sitting there in my apartment, I heard a familiar voice; it was distinctive and resonant. I soon recognized it as the voice of Ed Wittner, the music minister at Columbus Avenue Baptist Church in Waco. I listened through the paper thin walls as he shared the gospel of Jesus Christ with my neighbor, and I listened as my neighbor prayed and received Christ into his life. That night I wept in shame.

As a pastor, I led my people to give to the Lottie Moon Offering to reach the nations. I was so angry at my foreign neighbor for taking a twenty-five-cent newspaper that God had to bring another minister from the city to reach him.

We can either shout at sinners or show them the light. It will be difficult to do both.

Conclusion

We are saved into a church of members who devote themselves to worship, instruction, sharing, and evangelism. Let us be this kind of disciple so that we can make disciples who do the same. Whether or not we know it, we all need the community and encouragement the church provides.

The renowned preacher Fred Craddock tells the story of his father, who never went to church. When preachers came by and visited, Craddock's father gave them the standard line: "I know what you fellows down there at the church want. You want another name on the rolls, another pledge for the budget. Right? Isn't that the business you are in?" Craddock said he probably heard his dad say that a thousand times.

But one time his father didn't say it. It was the last time Fred saw his father alive. Afflicted with cancer, his father was in a Veteran's Administration hospital. He weighed barely seventy-four pounds. The breathing tube down his throat made it impossible for him to talk.

Flowers and potted plants filled the room. Even the table for meals was covered in flowers. Little cards were sprinkled throughout the flowers. Cards were stuck on the bulletin board. A stack of cards twenty inches deep sat beside the bed. Every one of these gifts came from the church: the men's Bible class; the women's fellowship; the children's department; the youth group. Every church organization imaginable had sent flowers with notes assuring Fred's dad of their love and prayers. Craddock's father saw Fred looking at all the cards and remembering all those things he used to say about the church.

Unable to talk, his father picked up a pencil and wrote on the side of the tissue box this line from *Hamlet*: "In this harsh world, draw your breath in pain and tell my story." Fred read the line and looked into his father's eyes, asking him what story he wanted told. His father took back the box and wrote out this confession: "I was wrong. I was wrong."[9]

As the little girl told the police officer, when we are lost and uncertain which way to go, we need to find our church. If we do, we can find our way home.[10] The church at its best has so much to offer. Christ invites us to invite others to join us in the community of the church. In the next chapter, we'll take a closer look at Christ's strategy for the proclamation of salvation.

CHAPTER *Eight*

Proclaiming the Message of Salvation

"And how can they hear without
someone preaching to them?"

—ROMANS 10:14

PREACH THE GOSPEL AT ALL times. If necessary use words."[1] In most cases, using words is necessary. In the Book of Acts, Luke tells us what Jesus continued to do and to teach through the community called the church. Jesus' followers huddled together in prayer, having learned the lesson of Gethsemane. When the promised Holy Spirit came at Pentecost, Peter proclaimed salvation powerfully, and the church expanded exponentially. We may learn from his invitation, "Save yourselves from this corrupt generation" (Acts 2:40). Three thousand accepted the message of the gospel and were baptized.

In Peter's sermon at Pentecost, he began to effectively fulfill Christ's personal commission to him to fish for people (Luke 5:10). This commission extended beyond Peter, however, to include all of

Jesus' disciples. Jesus sent out the Twelve (Luke 9:1–2), and the seventy-two (Luke 10:1) to go and proclaim the kingdom of God. After his resurrection, Jesus clarified this responsibility in what we call the Great Commission (Matthew 28:16–20):

> *Then the eleven disciples went to Galilee, to the mountain where Jesus had told them to go. When they saw him, they worshiped him; but some doubted. Then Jesus came to them and said, "All authority in heaven and on earth has been given to me. Therefore go and make disciples of all nations, baptizing them in the name of the Father and of the Son and of the Holy Spirit, and teaching them to obey everything I have commanded you. And surely I am with you always, to the very end of the age."*

The Greatest Power in the World

On the fateful day in May of 1997 when a tornado hit Cedar Park, Texas, I walked out of my office at New Hope First Baptist Church on my way to the hospital, looked up, and saw the funnel cloud. After warning the staff of the danger, I climbed in my car and headed south with the tornado in my rearview mirror. People are funny. With a tornado in our rearview mirrors, drivers stopped at all the stoplights. When I finally arrived at my house, I found our two sons running around in the yard, and I carried them inside where we waited for the storm to pass.

As the four of us crawled out of the tiny bathroom in which we had weathered the storm, I first heard that a local grocery store had been hit, and the roof had collapsed. Over the protests of my worried family, I headed out the door. Because it was still raining, I grabbed a yellow rain poncho out of the closet. After a circuitous route that took me down the back roads, I finally arrived at the store's parking lot. I put on my poncho and walked over to the grocery store. Crossing over yellow lines marking the disaster area and designed to keep out curiosity seekers, I walked up close to the front to see how I might help. I could see that the roof had caved in, but at that time nobody knew whether anybody was still trapped.

All the workers were wearing yellow ponchos. I joined a group, and we started talking about the storm and what we had seen. Over time, the conversation became friendlier, and everybody started looking at each other's identification on the ponchos to see who we were. Here was somebody from the fire department. Another was from the sheriff's department, and so on. Then one of them looked over and read the inscription on my poncho. I looked down, too, and in light blue I saw written boldly, "6 Flags." Then I remembered Bugs Bunny was on the back of my poncho. The looks on their faces asked, *By what authority exactly have you come across the yellow line?* I quickly explained that I was from New Hope First Baptist Church. A few blocks away, our steeple, silhouetted against the evening sky confirmed my story. They expressed thanks that the church was a shelter for displaced people. Still, I knew they doubted that cartoon characters and amusement parks could help with the destruction brought by the storm.

Surely Jesus addressed the doubt of his disciples when he began the Great Commission by describing the authority vested in him. "All authority in heaven and earth has been given to me" (Matt. 28:18). Jesus claims the corner on the authority market. He is *All Mighty*. As risen Lord, Jesus claims authority in both heaven and earth. There is no sphere where Jesus' comprehensive authority is limited. Dutch theologian Abraham Kuyper said it well, "There is not a single square inch of the entire cosmos of which Christ the sovereign Lord of all does not say, 'This is mine.'"[2]

More than the other Gospel writers, Matthew gave us a picture of this great authority. If we had to summarize the life and ministry of Jesus in a single word, perhaps it would be the word *authority*, in fact. Jesus *taught* with authority, *healed* with authority, and *forgave* sin with authority. Most of all, Jesus *lived* with authority.

Authority is the most striking and noticeable characteristic of Jesus' life. Both Jesus' friends and his foes noticed it. Jesus not only possessed authority, but he provided it to his disciples, sending them out with "authority" (Matt. 10:1). Later Jesus promised them the authority that comes with "the keys of the kingdom" (Matt. 16:19). Then Jesus sent his disciples into all of the world, offering them his authority to accomplish his purpose, with the promise that he would always be with them (Matt. 28:18–20).

Isn't it ironic that the one thing missing in many lives and ministries today is the very thing most evident in Jesus' ministry? We often minister as those without authority, going through the motions. But Jesus' promise of power still stands to all who are committed to Jesus' purpose and willing to receive his promise. While this idea offers little to those who are not serious about discipleship, it has everything to do with those who want to change the world. Imagine this: we have been authorized by the Author of life who *is* the authority and *gives* the authority we need to live authoritatively. We can live authoritatively, confident in Christ's ability and adequacy. All of our adequacy comes from him. We are never inadequate as long as we know that Christ's strength is perfected in our weakness (2 Corinthians 12:9).

Only when we recognize Christ's authority do we place ourselves in a position to receive it. When we recognize Jesus' authority, he transforms us.

Those who are content to live by their own authority likely never will recognize Jesus' greater authority. We might think that the devout religious leaders of Jesus' day would have been the first to recognize his power (Matt. 9:1–8). But when Jesus forgave a paralytic for his sins, the teachers of the law thought Jesus was usurping the high prerogative of God and accused him of blasphemy. Then Jesus explained before he healed the man, "But so that you may know that the Son of Man has authority in earth to forgive sins" (Matt. 9:6).

Later "the chief priests and the elders" asked, "By what authority are you doing these things?" (Matt. 21:23). Jesus refused to answer them. Instead he invited them to answer, *Was John the Baptist a prophet?* They were so concerned about protecting their own position that they refused to answer. Consequently, Jesus left them in their powerlessness. As long as they were satisfied with their own personal position, piety, prestige, and power, they would never be open to the power he had to offer them.

A ship captain looked into the dark night and saw faint lights in the distance. The lights appeared to be coming toward him across the water. Immediately he told his signalman to send a message: "Alter your course ten degrees south."

Promptly a return message was received: "Alter your course ten degrees north."

The captain was angered; his command had been ignored. So he sent a second message: "Alter your course ten degrees south—I am the captain!"

Soon another message was received: "Alter your course ten degrees north—I am Seaman Third Class Jones."

Immediately the captain sent a third message, knowing the fear it would evoke: "Alter your course ten degrees south—I am a battleship."

Then the reply came: "Alter your course ten degrees north—I am a lighthouse." Guess who yielded.

Are we willing to give up our authority in exchange for Christ's supremacy over our lives? Do we really want Christ's authority in our lives?

Only those who submit to Jesus' authority ever see his authority at work in the world. The crowd noticed after Jesus taught the Sermon on the Mount that he had authority unlike their religious leaders. They had heard others teach, but Jesus taught with unique authority (Matt. 7:28–29). We also see it in the temple guards, when the Pharisees sent them under their authority to arrest Jesus. When they returned without arresting Jesus, the temple guards' bosses, the chief priests and the Pharisees, asked in effect, *Why didn't you arrest him?* In effect they answered, *Arrest him? We were arrested by his words. We have heard you teach, but we never heard anybody speak as this man does* (John 7:45–46).

We see the same deference in the centurion (Matt. 8:8–13). Jesus offered to go and heal his servant. He answered, "I myself am a man under authority. . . ." Jesus was amazed by his faith.

Does our faith in Jesus' authority get his attention? Are we ever so surrendered and submitted that heaven says: *Now that is amazing.* The faith that pleases God is the faith that recognizes his authority and surrenders to Him. "To all who received him, to those who believed in his name, he gave the right to become the children of God" (John 1:12). If we recognize Jesus' authority, then we are in a position to receive it.

When we receive Christ's authority, he uses us to change the world. I have heard it said, *Without God, we cannot; without us, God will not.* This helps us understand Jesus' words, "You are the salt of the earth . . . you are the light of the world" (Matt. 5:13–14) We will be held responsible for the power Christ gives us. In Christ, God guarantees the Great Commission with all the authority needed to change the world.

A city faced great problems. The city council was in disarray; the council president and another councilman were headed to jail. In a panel discussion of community leaders, the panel moderator asked, *Whose fault is this?* Before anyone could answer, one of the panelists, a community and church leader, answered, *It's my fault.* All heads turned his way. He continued, *I have lived in this community for decades, and I am a Bible teacher. I should have been able to create an environment where what our council president did would have been unthinkable. You want someone to blame? I'll take the blame.*

Was he just grandstanding? No. Our presence in this world with Christ's power implies that we are going to make some substantial difference—like salt on food or light in darkness. If our world is bland, we are to season it. If it is rotting, we are to preserve it like salt preserves meat. If it is dark, we are to brighten and enlighten it. We must not take our salt and light and hide them as we complain about the insipid, rotten, dark world. God has given us authority. He expects us to use it.

A cartoon pictured a college student kneeling at the altar, with a cross in the background and a stained glass window behind it. The student prayed, "O Lord, the world is filled with people who are starving to death. O Lord, please feed the hungry." In the second panel, the student prayed, "O Lord, war is a sin, and it is destroying your world. O Lord, please stop all the wars on earth." In the third panel, the student is even more intense, down on all fours before the altar. "O Lord, he cried, "Prejudice is perhaps our worst sin. O Lord, please put an end to the conflict between the races and make us live as brothers." In the fourth panel, the scene has radically changed. A lightning bolt has pierced the altar, scattered the stones and knocked the college student to his back. With a look of astonishment on his face, the student heard the booming voice of God saying, "You do it!" Where is the authority to change the world—to feed the hungry, make peace, and end prejudice? In the church!

E. Stanley Jones (1884–1973), Methodist preacher and missionary, pointed out,

> Someone has said, "The early church did not say in dismay, 'Look what the world has come to,' but in delight, 'Look what has come to the world.'" They saw not merely the ruin, but the Resource for the reconstruction of that ruin. They saw not merely that sin did abound, but that grace did much more abound. On that assurance the pivot of history swung from blank despair, loss of moral nerve, and fatalism, to faith and confidence that at last sin had met its match. . . .[3]

Luke tells us they did it so well that the same scribes and Pharisees asked Peter and John, "By what power or what name did you do this?" (Acts 4:7). Further, "When they saw the courage of Peter and John and realized that they were unschooled, ordinary men, they were astonished and they took note that these men had been with Jesus" (Acts 4:13).

What is happening in our lives and churches that we could not do on our own? Have we become so content in our self-sufficiency, our power and abilities, that we think we no longer need Christ's? What will we do with the power God has given us? Jesus connected this power with his purpose. "But you will receive power when the Holy Spirit comes on you; and you will be my witnesses in Jerusalem, and in all Judea and Samaria, and to the ends of the earth" (Acts 1:8). Jesus' authority remains available to his people to accomplish a great purpose.

What could Jesus' authority look like in our lives and churches? Surely, we would stand confidently and testify boldly. These words are attributed to an unknown author, who may have faced persecution because of his faith:

> I am a part of the "Fellowship of the Unashamed." The die has been cast. The decision has been made. I have stepped over the line. I won't look back, let up, slow down, back away or be still. My past is redeemed, my

present makes sense, and my future is secure. I'm finished and done with low living, sight walking, small planning, smooth knees, colorless dreams, tamed visions, mundane talking, cheap giving and dwarfed goals.

I no longer need preeminence, prosperity, position, promotions, plaudits, or popularity. I don't have to be right, first, tops, recognized, praised, regarded, or rewarded. I now live by faith, lean on His presence, love with patience, lift by prayer, and labor with power.

My face is set, my gait is fast, my goal is heaven, my road is narrow, my way is rough, my companions are few, my Guide is reliable, and my mission is clear. I cannot be bought, compromised, detoured, lured away, turned back, deluded, or delayed. I will not flinch in the face of sacrifice, hesitate in the presence of adversity, negotiate at the table of the enemy, pander at the pool of popularity, or meander in the maze of mediocrity.

I won't give up, shut up, let up or slow up until I have stayed up, stored up, prayed up, paid up, and spoken up for the cause of Christ. I am a disciple of Jesus. I must go 'til He comes, give till I drop, preach 'til all know, and work 'til He stops me. And when He comes for His own, He will have no problem recognizing me. My banner is clear: I am a part of the "Fellowship of the Unashamed."

What if this testimony became ours?

The Greatest Purpose in the World

Given the great gift of power, the church now sets out to fulfill Christ's mission. How do we do it? In Matthew 28:19–20, Jesus mentioned four activities of the church: going, making disciples, baptizing, and teaching. Which is primary? Based on the order, we might assume that *going* is of paramount importance. Someone else might say, *Baptisms are the measure of a church.* Many of us might land squarely on the *teaching* mission of the church. But in all of these instances, we would miss the point. Although it is not obvious in some of our English translations, the verb "make disciples" is modified by the other three participles. Christ commissions the church with the primary purpose of *making disciples*. We make disciples as we go, baptize, and teach. Jesus' words greatly simplify our work and liberate us from a number of other good activities that might distract us from our one purpose of making disciples.

A disciple is a learner or an apprentice, a follower of Jesus Christ. Just as the Eleven had walked with Jesus and begun to become like him as they followed him, they were to lead others to do the same. For good or bad, we only make the same kinds of disciples we are. If we are mere admirers of Christ, we may invite others to do the same. Only if we are following Christ can we invite others as Paul did, "Follow my example, as I follow the example of Christ" (1 Corinthians 11:1).

For the second time in Matthew 28:19–20, Jesus used the word "all," in this instance to describe the scope of discipleship. Because Jesus has "all" authority, we are free to go to "all" nations. God has always cared about *all* people. To Israel God said through the prophet Isaiah, "It is too small a thing for you to be my servant to restore the tribes of Jacob and bring back those of Israel I have kept. I will also make you a light for the Gentiles that you may bring my salvation to the ends of the earth" (Isaiah 49:6). Fulfilling Jesus' greatest purpose, we are to make disciples of *all* nations. We begin to see the fulfillment of this at Pentecost when Jews of many nations became followers of Christ: "Parthians, Medes and Elamites; residents of Mesopotamia, Judea and Cappadocia, Pontus and Asia, Phrygia and Pamphylia, Egypt and the parts of Libya near Cyrene; visitors from Rome (both Jews and converts to Judaism); Cretans and Arabs" (Acts 2:9–11). The remainder of the Book of Acts shows the broadening witness of the church geographically and culturally in greater and greater concentric circles until Paul arrived in Rome.

Two millennia of missions work notwithstanding, we still have not completed the task of making disciples "of all the nations" (Matt. 28:19). To this day, unreached people and language groups in our world await the Christian witness. Paul clarified this need,

> *Everyone who calls on the name of the Lord will be saved. How then can they call on the one they have not believed in? And how can they believe in the one of whom they have not heard? And how can they hear*

without someone preaching to them? And how can they preach unless they are sent? (Romans 10:13–15).

From time to time, a well-intentioned believer will ask me, *Why do we spend money sending missionaries around the world? There is so much need in the United States.* If every religion were a means to relationship with God, this would greatly simplify the matter. Why not Islam for people in a certain geographic area, Buddhism and Hinduism for others, and other religions for other areas? Peter's answer to his critics provides our response, "Salvation is found in no one else [except Jesus Christ of Nazareth], for there is no other name given among men whereby we must be saved" (Acts 4:12).

Good news: the world is coming to where we live. A few years ago, Thong Lun and Mang Tiak, husband and wife, members of our church and chaplains in the Texas Medical Center, dreamed of starting a congregation for the Burmese people in Houston. They started with a small group of people. We had no way of knowing that political unrest in their homeland would soon bring a flood of Burmese people to Texas. Their congregation is now the fastest growing of all of Tallowood's congregations.

On the third anniversary of the establishment of their congregation, I preached as part of their worship service and then ate supper with them on our main campus. One young mother who had arrived as a refugee only a few days before our service held her three-year-old daughter tightly in her arms as she ate. The little girl only emerged from the safety of her mom's embrace to take a bite of food. Then she retreated quickly.

Eventually our volunteer army on the kitchen committee came around with little cups of ice cream. The little girl spied the ice cream warily, I presume because she had never seen anything like it before. When they gave her a taste, the sun rose on her face. She began to walk and then to dance around the room with her new discovery. I wept as I watched her. Although many people had been present in all of our services that morning, I realized that one of the best things we had done all day was give a cup of ice cream to a little girl from across the world. She and her family heard the gospel that day, and they will hear it again because of the faithfulness of Thong and Mang to love them and preach the gospel.

While we are committed to sending missionaries around the world through various missions-sending agencies, we must not neglect the call to the United States. A few years ago we went with the Tallowood choir to sing at Ground Zero in New York City and at the National Cathedral and on the Mall beside the Capitol in Washington, D. C. As our choir warmed up on one of the terraced lawns that cascade down from Congress to Union Station, my sons and I became thirsty. I went to find water. In the island circle in front of Union Station stood a man with a microphone and a small speaker. He was from Korea. As I listened, he preached the gospel in English with an accent, and then began to sing a familiar hymn,

> Redeemed, redeemed,
> Redeemed by the blood of the Lamb.
> Redeemed, redeemed,
> His child and forever I am.[4]

Years ago Baptists went to Korea with the gospel. Now God sent this brother as a missionary from Korea to the United States. He came to preach the same gospel we believe.

Does not God's great purpose liberate us from our xenophobia, our fear of and reaction against foreigners? As hundreds of thousands come to where we live from around the world, we must be prepared to share the gospel with every one of them. The government alone can resolve legal issues about immigration. Before the vigilante groups arrive at the border with guns, it would be good for Baptists to arrive with Bibles. Our work is to preach salvation to every person. Our goal must be to share the hope of Christ with every person in our community within their own language and context.

Going

Jesus also tells us *where* to make disciples. We are to make disciples *as we go*. Wherever we go, as we go, we make disciples. Christ's great purpose makes our movement meaningful. Whether we are going to school or on a trip around the world, we go for Christ.

On occasion, our going takes us on an intentional short-term missions trip. How do we measure the success of these trips? We have asked our church to evaluate the results not only in the places we go but also in the lives of those who go. Anyone can count the seeds in an apple. But only God can count the apples in a seed. We become Christ's seeds planted everywhere we go. God will produce great fruit through us as we are faithful to make disciples as we go. For this reason, we might consider ourselves to be on a short-term missions project for the rest of our lives. We are always on mission.

Baptizing

What difference does baptism make in salvation? First, we must see that Christ commands baptism as part of the process of making disciples. We often encounter people who have been believers in Christ for many years but were never baptized. Baptism is an important ordinance that Christ has given to the church. It is a symbol not only of cleansing but more importantly of identification with Christ in his burial and resurrection. "We were therefore buried with him through baptism into death in order that, just as Christ was raised from the dead through the glory of the Father, we too may live a new life" (Rom. 6:4).

Does one have to be baptized to become a Christian? True, the thief on the cross was not baptized and yet Christ promised him a place in paradise (Luke 23:43). As we have emphasized in earlier chapters, salvation is by grace through faith. Baptism becomes a symbol of this inward transformation. Christ gives us new life at the moment of salvation; baptism provides a powerful portrait of the gift of salvation. We should not, therefore, use the word *just* with the word *symbol* in this case. A symbol is as powerful as the truth it represents. The ring on the third finger of my left hand is a symbol of the marriage commitment I made twenty-five years ago. True, the ring is not the same as my marriage, but it tells everyone I meet that I am committed to Melanie. In the same way baptism must not be minimized. It represents our identification with the resurrection of Jesus Christ.

Baptists have historically taught believers' baptism by immersion. We mean by this that only believers should be baptized. This teaching contrasts with that of those who baptize infants as a means of salvation or with what is called *covenant* baptism before those being baptized are old enough to understand. In Acts 2:39, Peter preached, "The promise is for you and your children. . . ." Luke made crystal clear two verses later, "Those who accepted his message were baptized" (Acts 2:41). How can an infant accept the message of salvation? The Ethiopian eunuch chose baptism only after he understood the death of Christ and committed himself to become a follower of Jesus (Acts 8:36–39). Based on biblical teachings such as these, we see baptism as a step of obedience that follows the actual commitment of the individual to Christ.

The dedication of children to the Lord is a decision by parents to give thanks for the life of the child and to consecrate their home as a place where the child may come to know Christ. Nevertheless, we must not confuse the dedication of children with baptism in the New Testament, which is clearly taught as a matter of obedience for believers.

Our culture presses children to grow up faster and faster. This decision to follow Christ must be allowed to take deep root in the life of a child. For this reason, I advocate waiting to baptize children until we sense they understand more than just that they want to be baptized. They must understand sin and repentance and the crucifixion and resurrection before they can follow Christ in discipleship and baptism.

At what age are they ready? It is different for each child, but it must not be hurried. One woman asked me to baptize her three-year-old daughter. When I explained that I would not do that, she told me another church would. I pressed further to discover that she feared that she herself might become gravely ill and die before her child had the opportunity to become a believer. This baptism would give the mother assurance of her whole family being Christians. I carefully and caringly explained to her that her child was safe in God's keeping until such time that she could understand and receive Christ for herself. Our church has established a regular new Christian's class for children to help to ensure that they understand clearly their commitment to Christ.

We baptize "in the name of the Father and of the Son and of the Holy Spirit" (Matt. 28:19). The expression "in the name of" clarifies the basis of authority. Believers are baptized with the full imprimatur of the triune God. As an alternative, some denominations focus on the expression, "in the name of Jesus Christ for the forgiveness of your sins" (Acts 2:38). This expression does not contradict or correct the teaching of the Great Commission—"in the name of the Father and of the Son and of the Holy Spirit." Some of Peter's listeners may have received baptism or cleansing as they became proselytes to Judaism. Others might have received baptism for the repentance of sins by John the Baptist. Peter clarified again that Jesus' name alone offers forgiveness. The fuller expression of Father, Son, and Holy Spirit includes and encompasses Peter's teaching in Acts 2:38.

Why do Baptists practice baptism by immersion? The Greek word *baptizo* literally means *to submerge under water*. The practice of sprinkling or pouring fails to capture the full sense of this word. Further, immersion pictures beautifully the image of being buried with Christ and raised to new life in a way that other modes cannot. From the beginning, immersion after one becomes a believer has marked Baptists' quest for a regenerate membership.

Teaching

The third action of the church in making disciples is "teaching them to obey everything I have commanded you" (Matt. 28:20). We must teach to make disciples. The *save them and strand them* approach of some evangelistic efforts falls far short of Christ's teaching. It is good to evangelize and baptize, but without teaching we invite new believers to a truncated discipleship.

When we arrived to serve at Tallowood in 1998, our younger son Chase was about to start kindergarten. He informed his Sunday School teacher after his first class that he would not return. When his curious teacher asked him the reason, Chase explained, "We have the Jesus video at home, and I have already seen all of this stuff." Of course, he has been in Sunday School ever since. His attitude, however, was not unlike the believer who receives Christ and says, *I already know all I need to know.* The process of growing as a disciple calls for continued learning for a lifetime.

Our Lord further commissioned the church to comprehensive instruction—"teaching them to obey *everything I have commanded you*" (italics added for emphasis). This is why we need systematic exposition of Scripture. In our worship and in our Bible study classes, we must study the Scripture text. We must hold in balance the revelation of Scripture and its relevance in our lives. We should never compromise revelation on the altar of relevance. For that matter, revelation is inherently relevant. What God said in the Scriptures still matters today.

Stuart Briscoe, author and long-time pastor of Elmbrook Church in Brookfield, Wisconsin, tells about traveling to Poland for several weeks of ministry during the Cold War. One winter day his sponsors drove him in the dead of night to the middle of nowhere. When Briscoe walked into a dilapidated building crammed with 100 young people, he realized it was a unique opportunity. Through an interpreter he preached from John 15 on *abiding in Christ.* Ten minutes into his message, the lights went out. The room went pitch black. His interpreter urged him to keep talking. Unable to see his notes or read his Bible, he continued. After he had preached in the dark for twenty minutes, the lights suddenly blinked on, and what he saw startled him: everyone was on their knees, and they remained there for the rest of his message. The next day he commented on this occurrence to a person present. The person said, "After you left, we stayed on our knees most of the night. Your teaching was new to us. We wanted to make sure we were abiding in Christ."[5] This story reminds us of the new believers in the church at Berea—"Now the Bereans were of more noble character than the Thessalonians, for they received the message with great eagerness and examined the Scriptures every day to see if what Paul said was true" (Acts 17:11).

What are we to teach? We are to teach disciples to obey. The life of following Christ is not the life of doing whatever we desire after we are baptized. Instead we are called to take upon ourselves *the discipline of discipleship.* This expression further captures the third of the four *all* expressions in the Great Commission. "Obey everything" is literally *obey all things.* Such teaching must therefore be comprehensive. We must teach all of the commands of Jesus to these new believers. What did Christ command? When asked to identify the greatest commandment in the law, Jesus responded, "Love the Lord your God with all your heart and with all your soul and with all your mind. This is the first and greatest commandment. And the second is like it: Love your neighbor as yourself. All the Law and the Prophets hang on these two commandments" (Matt. 22:37–40). Jesus' instruction to teach "them to obey everything" he commanded was not a call to establish a new legalism or Pharisaism or bibliolatry. Rather, obeying Christ follows from and confirms our experience of salvation *by* Christ.

The Greatest Promise in the World

What, we may wonder, is Christ doing while we are using his great power to fulfill his great purpose? He is keeping his great promise to us. "And surely I am with you always to the very end of the age" (Matt. 28:20). This promise instills great confidence in us.

When is Christ with us? "Always." Here we find the fourth use of the word *all* in this passage. The promise is specific, literally *all the days* in the Greek. It is not just that Christ will be with us eternally, but each and every day, at all times, he will be with us. Paul later stated that nothing in all creation "will be able to separate us from the love of God that is in Christ Jesus our Lord" (Rom. 8:39).

Ten days before her marriage, Lillian Thrasher went to hear a missionary speak. Before the day was over, she broke her engagement and made the decision to become a missionary in Egypt. There were no formal missionary appointments in her denomination, and so Lillian Thrasher, a single adult, gathered her money and possessions and headed for a missionary convention in Pittsburgh. She was confident that God would provide the opportunity and the finances for passage to Egypt. God did not disappoint. As a missionary in Egypt in the early twentieth century, she gave her attention particularly to babies and their mothers. When one of the mothers died, Lillian insisted on keeping the baby. Her missionary supervisor in Cairo ordered her to take the baby back. In response, Lillian started an orphanage. During her five decades in Egypt, Lillian provided for more than 8,000 orphans and widows. Her prayer was simply this, "O God, since you have enabled me to do the simple things I can do, I have full trust in you to do the great things which I cannot."[6] God is with us!

When will this great power for this great purpose with this great promise come to a conclusion? Jesus' words remind us that this age will come to an end eventually. Until then Jesus reminds us that while we use his great power for his great purpose we will experience his great presence. Trusting this promise changes everything.

My friend Shawn Shannon who serves at the University of Mary Hardin-Baylor has an excellent answer when I ask her, "How are you doing?" She simply explains, "I am sustained." This is who we are: sustained by our Sustainer and his strength. God always keeps his promises.

CHAPTER Nine

Blessed Assurance

"For I am convinced that neither death nor
life, neither angels nor demons, neither the
present nor the future, nor any powers, neither
height nor depth, nor anything else in all
creation, will be able to separate us from the
love of God that is in Christ Jesus our Lord."

—ROMANS 8:38–39

HAVE YOU HEARD ABOUT THE man who awakened one morning and realized he was tired of shaving his beard? On a whim, he decided to break the old routine. In the movies, he had seen men go to the barber shop for warm lather and a shave. When he went to the local barber shop, the receptionist asked, "What do you need?"

"I need a shave," he responded.

The receptionist invited him to be seated in a barber's chair and told him, "Grace will be right with you."

Soon a woman named Grace came, shook his hand, put the lather on his face, and proceeded to give him the shave to end all shaves. She shaved him closely without a single nick or cut. He thanked her and asked how much he owed her. "$100," she answered.

"$100?" He winced at the price, but he paid her and chalked it up to experience.

The next morning the man awakened, walked to the mirror as usual, and realized to his surprise that his face was still smooth. On the third day, he was amazed to discover the same thing. After some days passed, the fact that he hadn't needed to shave began to bother him. So he went back to the barber shop. He said, "I don't understand. You have to explain this to me. I received a shave here, and now I no longer need to shave."

The owner smiled at him and said, "Don't worry. You've been shaved by Grace. Once shaved, always shaved!"

As silly as it may sound to be shaven once for all, even more strange to some is the idea that once we are saved, we will always be saved. Did you know that the Bible never actually uses the expression *once saved, always saved*? So what exactly does the Bible teach? Can we have any assurance of our salvation? How can we know where we will spend eternity?

Let's Begin with Definitions

The expression *once saved, always saved* speaks of the assurance of salvation forever once one has been saved. One cannot *lose one's salvation*. The words *eternal security* or *the security of the believer* express a related, similar thought. The person who has experienced salvation is secure in that salvation eternally.

Two other important expressions emerge from our study of this subject in the Scriptures. *Assurance* means we can be sure of our salvation. The First Letter of John reads like a tract on the subject of assurance.[1] John wrote to the first-century Christians,

> And this is the testimony: God has given us eternal life, and this life is in his Son. He who has the Son has life; he who does not have the Son of God does not have life. I write these things to you who believe in the name of the Son of God so that you may know that you have eternal life (1 John 5:11–13).

The writer of Hebrews expressed it this way, "let us draw near to God with a sincere heart in full assurance of faith. . ." (Hebrews 10:22).[2] Paul used the same Greek word translated "assurance" to describe the "deep conviction" believers received along with the power of the gospel and the Holy Spirit (1 Thessalonians 1:5). God's presence provides assurance. Paul described the same promise in another letter as the "full riches of complete understanding" (Colossians 2:2).

A fourth expression is *the perseverance of the saints.* Remember that the term *saint* in the New Testament describes every believer in or follower of Christ. Those who are truly *saints* persevere. "You need to persevere so that when you have done the will of God you will receive what he has promised" (Heb. 10:36). In the end, believers will remain true to Christ and receive his promise. In other words, those who truly come to Christ by faith will not fall away but continue in a state of grace eternally.[3]

The alternative view advocates the idea of *apostasy* or *falling away from grace.* Some root this idea in the choice of a person to walk away from Christ after walking with him. Others view this idea more legalistically, seeing each sin as a possible departure from grace, so that if sinners died in the moment after they sinned, they would be lost for eternity. What can we learn from the Scriptures on this subject?

Evidence for the Perseverance of the Saints

Sincere believers cite Scriptures both for and against the doctrine of eternal security. All agree that Jesus said, "He who stands firm to the end will be saved" (Mark 13:13). On what basis do Christians find the strength to persevere to the finish? Salvation is God's work from beginning to end. If we contributed to salvation by our works, then we might lose our salvation when we stopped doing those works. However, we believe that salvation is by grace through faith. If we cannot do anything to save ourselves, then we cannot do anything to lose that salvation.

We find assurance of our perseverance in the words of our Savior:

All that the Father gives me will come to me and whoever comes to me,
I will never drive away. For I have come down from heaven not to do my
will but to do the will of him who sent me. And this is the will of him
who sent me, that I shall lose none of all that he has given me, but raise
them up at the last day. For my Father's will is that everyone who looks
to the Son and believes in him shall have eternal life, and I will raise him
up at the last day (John 6:37–40).

We believe that Christians will persevere not because of our own strength but because of the faithfulness of the God in whom we trust. Our faith is as strong as its object, Christ. We also trust in God's great promises and in God's presence revealed in the Holy Spirit. In fact, the New Testament teaches that our assurance and security are all wrapped up in the faithfulness of the triune God—Father, Son, and Holy Spirit.

God's Role in Perseverance

Before January 15, 2009, hardly anyone knew the name "Captain Sully." A heroic moment changed everything for this airline pilot. When birds destroyed both of his plane's engines in flight, Chesley B. "Sully" Sullenberger III guided a crippled US Airways jetliner safely into the Hudson River, saving all 155 people aboard.[4] Captain Sully became an instant hero. His decision and skill saved the lives of the people on the plane. None of the passengers came out of the plane saying, *I helped the captain save our lives.* In a similar way, the Scriptures make clear that our security and safety as believers rests in the hands of the great Captain of our salvation, Jesus Christ (Heb. 2:10). Christ alone has the power to save us, and Christ alone will.

Salvation is a relationship in which God knows us and we know God. Jesus said,

My sheep listen to my voice; I know them, and they follow me. I give
them eternal life and they shall never perish; no one can snatch them
out of my hand. My Father who has given them to me is greater than

*all; no one can snatch them out of my Father's hand. I and the Father
are one (John 10:27–30).*

Not only does God choose to know us, but God also offers eternal life as a gift. Once this gift is received, believers discover that we are in Christ's hand, which is in the Father's hand.

When our sons were little and we walked in an area of heavy traffic, cars racing by inches from the sidewalk, I just put my hand out and said, "It's up to you, boys. If you hold on you live. If you let go, you die." Of course not. I did not leave their safety to chance. Children might dart out into traffic as I did years ago and be hit by a truck. No. My children's safety rested not in their ability to hold on to me but in my ability to hold on to them.

Do we have any idea how strong God's grip is? Someone once allegedly requested at an evangelistic meeting that they sing the song, "God's Grip Don't Slip." The title is grammatically awkward but theologically accurate! Better still is the hymn title, "O Love That Wilt Not Let Me Go"[5]

As previous chapters in this book emphasize, our salvation experience leads us to do good things for God. But the good things we do cannot secure or maintain our relationship with God. An example emerges from Jesus' words in the Sermon on the Mount,

> *Not everyone who says to me, "Lord, Lord," will enter the kingdom of heaven, but only he who does the will of my Father who is in heaven. Many will say to me on that day, "Lord, Lord, did we not prophesy in your name and in your name drive out demons and perform many miracles?" Then I will tell them plainly, "I never knew you. Away from me you evildoers" (Matt. 7:21–23, italics added for emphasis).*

It is not that the Lord knew them and forgot about them. Rather there never was a relationship in the first place. Without a relationship there is no salvation and no security. These did not lose salvation. They never had it in the first place.

Paul, too, explained the security of salvation in terms of God's work on our behalf. God finishes what God starts. How inspiring are

Paul's words to the Philippians, "Being confident of this, that he who began a good work in you will carry it on to completion until the day of Christ Jesus" (Philippians 1:6). In this single verse we see the picture of salvation. God begins the work, continues the work, and completes the work.

From God's point of view the work of salvation in the life of a believer is guaranteed to go to completion. Confidently Paul wrote, "And we know that in all things God works for the good of those who love him, who have been called according to his purpose" (Rom. 8:28). Paul spoke of certainties, "And we know. . . ." God who is working for good has already called believers according to his purpose. He foreknew us and predestined us to be conformed to the likeness of his Son (Rom. 8:29). Paul placed the whole act of salvation from start to finish in the past tense as a completed act: "And those he predestined, he also called; those he called he also justified; those he justified he also glorified" (Rom. 8:30).

Not only has God done all of this for us, but God also continues to work actively on our behalf. Christ's death, resurrection, and ongoing intercession underscore the certainty of the completion of God's will in our lives. Nothing ever separates us from God's love. Paul offered a comprehensive list of the forces that might separate Christians from God's love (Rom. 8:37–38). He concluded that none of these things, "nor anything else in all creation, will be able to separate us from the love of God" (Rom. 8:39).

As Paul wrote to the believers at Corinth about his responsibility for ministry, he shed further light on the issue. Using the metaphor of building a house to describe ministry, he wrote, "But each one should be careful how he builds. For no one can lay any foundation other than the one already laid, which is Jesus Christ" (1 Cor. 3:10–11). Christ personally provides the only sure foundation of salvation for every person. One can build on that foundation with good materials or poor materials. On the Day of Judgment, fire will reveal the quality of the work. What if one builds with gold, silver, and costly stones? That person will receive a reward. On the other hand if that person builds with wood, hay, or stubble, the work will be consumed and lost. "If it is burned up, he will suffer loss; he himself will be saved but only as one escaping through the flames" (1 Cor. 3:15). Even if a believer wastes time in meaningless ministry, the believer's salvation is not lost, because it cannot be lost. Paul went on to show the Corinthians they were God's temple. If one were to destroy God's temple, God would destroy him (1 Cor. 3:16–17). One might lose physical life but not be lost for eternity.[6]

God guards the salvation God has given. Paul affirmed his personal assurance again in his final letter to Timothy, "I know whom I have believed, and am convinced that he is able to guard what I have entrusted to him for that day" (2 Tim. 1:12). God has sealed this salvation by his own presence through the Holy Spirit of promise until the day of redemption (Eph.1:13; 4:30). This same Spirit 'helps us in our weakness," by interceding "for us with groans that words cannot express. And he who searches our hearts knows the mind of the Spirit, because the Spirit intercedes for the saints in accordance with God's will" (Rom. 8:26–27).

Not only has God purposed to complete our salvation and guaranteed it by his Holy Spirit, but also Jesus himself intercedes for us. Speaking of our great High Priest, the Book of Hebrews affirms, "Therefore he is able to save completely those who come to God through him, because he always lives to intercede for them" (Heb. 7:25). Further, 1 John states, "My dear children, I write this to you so that you will not sin. But if anybody does sin, we have one who speaks to the Father in our defense—Jesus Christ, the Righteous One. He is the atoning sacrifice for our sins, and not only for ours but also for the sins of the whole world" (1 John 2:1–2).

God's faithfulness assures our perseverance. Theologian Michael Green states, "Though a man may fall into grievous sin, though he may appear to fall away entirely, he cannot be utterly lost, or the death of Christ and the promise and the purpose of God would be frustrated."[7] In summary, our faithful Father purposes to complete his work of salvation, sealing it by his Spirit, who along with the Son intercedes for us on the basis of his completed work on the cross, atoning for our sins. Clearly, we find strong evidence supporting the assurance that believers will persevere. Let's consider some further evidence in the lives of believers themselves.

Evidence of Perseverance in the Lives of Believers

Have you ever doubted your salvation? During my youth, a member of my family struggled mightily with the assurance of her salvation. Although she believed Christians cannot lose their salvation, she was not convinced she was a believer.

Granting that salvation is God's work from beginning to end, how do we know whether we ourselves have really experienced that salvation? At one level, we declare the reality of our faith by persevering in relationship with God. The fact that we are still walking with God means we are believers.

We return to the small but powerful letter of 1 John to find further evidence that reveals the truth about our relationship with Christ. *First, we know we are followers of Christ if we believe and live the truth.* "But you have an anointing from the Holy One, and all of you know the truth" (1 John 2:20). What do followers of Christ believe? We must believe that Jesus Christ has come in the flesh (1 John 4:2), is the Savior of the world (1 John 4:14), and is the One who loves us with an undying love (1 John 4:16). This belief, as we have shown, must be more than cognitive assent. "No one can say, 'Jesus Christ is Lord,' except by the Holy Spirit" (1 Cor. 12:3). Our true confession of Christ or profession of faith reveals the authenticity of our faith.

Further, our conduct confirms our confession. Believers obey Christ. "We know that we have come to know him if we obey his commands. . . . Whoever claims to live in him must walk as Jesus did" (1 John 2:3, 6). So we live lives of righteousness and discontinue known sin (1 John 2:29; 3:6). This is not to say that a believer never sins again. It does, however, affirm that the normative pattern for a follower of Christ is uncomfortableness with sinful behavior. Believers reveal our relationship by the fruit we bear in our lives.

Also, authentic followers of Christ love one other. "Whoever loves his brother lives in the light, and there is nothing in him to make him stumble. But whoever hates his brother is in darkness. . ." (1 John 2:10–11).[8] The acceptance and accountability we need to live the Christian life are found in the Christian community we call the church. Recognizing the importance of relationships, John stated bluntly, "If anyone says, 'I love God,' yet hates his brother, he is a liar. For anyone who does not love his brother, whom he has seen, cannot love God, whom he has not seen. And he has given us this command: Whoever loves God must also love his brother" (1 John 4:20–21).

Objections to Eternal Security

Have you ever been certain a person was a believer in Christ, only to discover later that that the person denied any relationship with Christ? How does this experience comport with the doctrine of perseverance of the saints? Some who question the teaching of the perseverance of the saints cite New Testament passages that seem to say apostasy is a possibility for believers.

Those who object to perseverance might say, *If God gives us the freedom to choose Christ, then God gives us the freedom to reject him as well.* Does the doctrine of perseverance or eternal security limit the freedom of humankind? Based on what we have seen in the Scriptures, we can respond, *If God can give us faith without violating our freedom, God can also keep us saved without disrupting our freedom.*[9]

A second objection to perseverance is the laxness with which many believers claim *once saved always saved.* Does assurance of salvation lead a person to spiritual laziness at best and sin at worst? As an analogy, if I ran no risk of becoming overweight, wouldn't I just eat ice cream all of the time? (My official answer to that is *yes.*) In regard to the original question—Does assurance of salvation lead a person to spiritual laziness at best and sin at worst?—the answer is *no.* The transformation Christ brings in our lives through regeneration and continues through sanctification makes a true believer in Christ ultimately uncomfortable with sin. Indeed, if a person lived as to demonstrate a complete rejection of Christ, we might wonder whether that person ever believed in Christ in the first place. As it sometimes used to be stated, *Faith that fizzles before the finish was flawed from the first.* Failure to persevere would be a sign the person never had the seed of faith in the first place.

A third objection to perseverance focuses on the examples of supposed apostates. What about Judas Iscariot (Matt. 27:1–5) and

Ananias (Acts 5:1–11)? Although these men had an appearance of relationship with Christ, there was no true inward transformation. This passage in 1 John can be applied to them: "They went out from us, but they did not really belong to us. For if they had belonged to us, they would have remained with us; but their going showed that none of them belonged to us" (1 John 2:19). Those who have real relationship with God, like David and Peter, repent of their sin and return to God.[10]

A fourth objection claims the Scriptures teach apostasy or falling from grace. What does the Bible actually teach? Certainly there are passages that teach that persevering faith is essential to our final deliverance from sin. Jesus stated, "But he who stands firm to the end will be saved" (Matt. 24:13; Mark 13:13). Paul added, "By this gospel you are saved, if you hold firmly to the word I preached to you. Otherwise, you have believed in vain (1 Cor. 15:2). In Jesus' letters to the seven churches in Revelation he offered great promises "to him who overcomes. . ." (Rev. 2:7, 11, 17, 26; 3:5, 12, 21).

Such passages might be taken to indicate that one could have faith and yet not persevere. However, as Baptist theologian W. T. Conner stated, "The salvation of a man elected to salvation is from all eternity certain in the mind and purpose of God, yet it is conditioned upon faith . . . that perseveres and conquers."[11] Other passages demonstrate that perseverance in faith confirms regeneration in our lives. Paul wrote, ". . . I beat my body and make it my slave so that after I have preached to others, I myself will not be disqualified for the prize" (1 Cor. 9:27). Hebrews uses the expression, "if we hold firmly" (Heb. 3: 14; 4:14; see 3:6). Those who have only a superficial and temporary faith fall away because they were never really believers (Matt. 13:20–21; 2 Peter 2:20–22).

We also find Scriptures that show a marked lack of development in the life of a believer. Perhaps most prominent among these is a passage from the Book of Hebrews. "It is impossible for those who have once been enlightened, who have tasted the heavenly gift, who have shared in the Holy Spirit, who have tasted the goodness of the word of God and the powers of the coming age, if they fall away to be brought back to repentance. . ." (Heb. 6:4–6). In context, these verses speak about believers who have not grown spiritually to maturity. They should have become teachers serving others, but they could tolerate only milk instead of solid food themselves (Heb. 5:12–14). The writer concluded that he was confident of better things in their case, "things that accompany salvation" (Heb. 6:9). Does this passage teach apostasy? Options for interpretation include first that the writer was making a hypothetical argument: "If it were possible for one to fall away, that one could not be renewed to repentance."[12] Another interpretation is that these were people who had publicly confessed allegiance to Christ and then subsequently repudiated their relationship with him.[13] They were never truly believers, however. Other commentators say this person is only "in danger of being cursed" (Heb. 6:8).

We should not minimize the seriousness of Hebrews 6:4–6. It is a real warning emphasizing a real danger. In the name of *once saved, always saved*, nobody should justify sinful behavior or trivialize the holiness of God. On the other hand, we should not exaggerate the importance of our failures as though every sin results in the loss of salvation. Ultimately these verses must be interpreted in the light of the remainder of the New Testament, which clearly affirms the security of salvation through the power of the God who saves us.

It is possible for one who claims to be a Christian to stop following Christ. The Scriptures affirm that possibility, and people have done so. The question is, *Were they ever believers in the first place?* Or were they like Simon the sorcerer in Acts 8:13, impostors who were baptized and blessed as followers only to demonstrate later that they never knew Christ at all (see Matt.7:22).

Further, using Hebrews 6:4–6 to say we can lose our salvation and regain it misses the point of the passage. Hebrews says clearly that those who, in my view, pretend faith and then walk away denying Christ cannot be restored to Christ. To reject Christ in our lives, refusing to be a child of God when we have the opportunity, may very well set forth a pattern for eternity that will not be revoked. It would be a grave mistake to put off choosing Christ in favor of some sin, with the idea that at any moment we may change course and receive Christ. "Today, if you hear his voice, do not harden your hearts" (Heb. 3:7, 15; 4:7).

The Benefits and Dangers of Assurance

What difference does assurance make in our lives? In a word, *everything*. To know that we are followers of Christ and safe in him, far from encouraging sin brings a deep sense of gratitude resulting in godly behavior.

In any congregation there might be three types of people present. First, *some are secure but not sure.* These are people who have authentically trusted in Christ so that they are secure in Christ but they are never quite sure about it. They may doubt their goodness and consequently doubt God's goodness. They may honestly wonder whether people like themselves could really be saved. They doubt their own intentions. Unfortunately, this doubt paralyzes them instead of empowering them. The result is that they never really live up to their spiritual potential. They live with the fear that they have gone one sin too far. In their minds they never know which sin rules them out of the kingdom. Is it the thousandth? or the ten thousandth? Who is keeping count?

In our churches, second, there might also be people who are absolutely sure they are saved but are not really secure because they never really had a relationship with Jesus Christ. *They possess a false assurance.* Should not we be concerned about those who went through the motions but never loved God? What if all they want from God is *fire insurance* from an eternity in hell? Having sought it they mistakenly believe they are going to heaven regardless of what they do.

A third group may be *people who are truly secure in their salvation.* They are really saved, and they are also sure of that salvation. Even though they may doubt their own goodness, they never doubt God's.

For a season, while we were attempting to gain custody of the little girl we recently adopted (see chapter 5), she lived at the Texas Baptist Children's Home in Round Rock, Texas. In Cottage One, under the loving care of Mom and Pop Toner, Casey learned what it means to be loved by perfect strangers. One night before she went to bed, she asked for a banana to eat. That very night she had eaten seven helpings of beef stroganoff (which she says is the best in the world). Still she claimed to be hungry.

"You can't be hungry," said one house parent.

"But if I had a banana, I could go to sleep," she explained. Ultimately, the parent let her go and get a banana. Banana in hand, she was able to rest.

Casey's story reminded me of some children in Europe after World War II. These abandoned and orphaned children had difficulty resting at night. On further investigation, the caregivers learned that the children could not sleep because they were afraid they would not have food the next day. The anxiety kept them awake. Finally, the orphanage determined to place a piece of bread in the hands of the children each night. Knowing that their next meal was secure, they could sleep.

In a similar way, the Lord's Supper reminds us of our security in Christ. Christ's body and Christ's blood are enough for us in this uncertain world. What God wants for us is that we should be able to rest secure in the knowledge that the One who has provided our salvation is well able to preserve it.

> Blessed Assurance, Jesus is mine!
> Oh, what a foretaste of glory divine!
> Heir of salvation, purchase of God,
> Born of His Spirit, washed in His blood
>
> This is my story, this is my song,
> Praising my Savior all the day long![14]

CHAPTER *Ten*

Toward Salvation's Glorious Completion

"But we know that when he appears, we shall
be like him, for we shall see him as he is."

—1 JOHN 3:2

I F YOU DIED TONIGHT, *would you go to heaven or to hell?* With appreciation for the intention of the question, I wonder how this form of evangelism has shaped our understanding of salvation. Is salvation only about our eternal destiny?

Salvation is not only about getting into heaven but about heaven getting into us. When heaven gets into us, we grow in anticipating a glorious consummation of our relationship with God. A day will come when finally we will be victorious in our battle against sin. The victory of Christ over the powers of sin and death, which we have already begun to experience here, will be completed in us. The word Bible scholars use most often to describe the consummation of salvation is *glorification*. The Scriptures frequently use the word *glorify*

146

to describe our worship of God. Just imagine the amazing grace of our God who purposes to glorify his children as we glorify him for eternity.

In fact, we have seen that Paul describes glorification as something that has already begun from God's point of view, "Those he justified, he also glorified" (Romans 8:30). In another letter, Paul also spoke of glorification as a process taking place in the present, "And we who with unveiled faces all reflect the Lord's glory, are being transformed into his likeness with ever-increasing glory, which comes from the Lord, who is the Spirit" (2 Corinthians 3:18).

Even so, this process of glorification also promises a future revelation: God wants the glory he has shared with his Son to be revealed in us until we ultimately become like Christ. Paul wrote, "Now if we are children then we are heirs—heirs of God and co-heirs with Christ, if indeed we share in his sufferings in order that we may also share in his glory. I consider that our present sufferings are not worth comparing with the glory that will be revealed in us" (Rom. 8:17–18).

Our Glorious King

Do we ever contemplate our glorious God? In the Old Testament, God identifies himself by revealing his glory. The Hebrew word for *glory* is *kabod*. The word speaks of weight and substance that reflect importance.[1] Our God is a substantial and stalwart God. He led his people out of Egypt with a cloud by day and a pillar of fire by night. Later, when Moses boldly asked God to reveal his glory, God passed by, first putting Moses in the cleft of the rock and covering him there with his hand (Exodus 33:18).

The New Testament uses the word *doxa* to describe Jesus' glory. The word speaks of the honor resulting from a good reputation.[2] On the Mount of Transfiguration, Jesus' "face shone like the sun, and his clothes became as white as light" (Matthew 17:2). Jesus later explained that when he returned in the Second Coming, "They will see the Son of Man coming on the clouds of the sky with power and great glory" (Matt. 24:30). When John saw Jesus in his vision on the

Isle of Patmos, Jesus' "head and hair were white like wool, as white as snow, and his eyes were like blazing fire. His feet were like bronze glowing in a furnace. . . . His face was like the sun shining in all its brilliance" (Revelation 1:14–16). John caught a glimpse of the glory of our King.

In our discussions and questions about heaven, we often focus on the place. But Jesus invites us to focus on him. The best part of heaven and the best thing about eternity will be our uninterrupted communion with Jesus. Jesus spoke to his disciples on the night before he was crucified to calm their fears and comfort them in the events that would transpire. "Do not let your hearts be troubled. Trust in God. Trust also in me" (John 14:1). Before Jesus ever explained that his Father's house had many rooms, he wanted them to trust him. In fact, Jesus' description of heaven centers strongly in the promise of his presence. Note in John 14:2–7 how Jesus pointed to himself as the source of comfort and hope:

> In my Father's house are many rooms; if it were not so I would have told you. I am going there to prepare a place for you. And if I go and prepare a place for you, I will come back to take you to be with me that you also may be where I am. You know the way to the place where I am going. . . . I am the way and the truth and the life. No one comes to the Father except through me. If you really knew me, you would know my Father as well. From now on, you do know him and have seen him (John 14:2–7).

Our little girl recently had the opportunity to buy various messages that attach to her new bottle-cap necklace. There were initials and cute sayings from which to choose. One inscription said, "It's all about me." When I came home from work, she explained, "I didn't buy that because it is not right. It is not all about us. It is all about God."

Both earth and heaven are all about God. Jesus left his glory and lived here to glorify his Father, but a time came when he returned to his glory. In Jesus' high priestly prayer on the night before his crucifixion, he began with the petition for mutual glorification: "Father, the time has come. Glorify your Son, that your Son may glorify you" (John 17:1). He continued this theme, "I have brought you glory on earth by completing the work you gave me to do. And now, Father, glorify me in your presence with the glory I had with you before the world began" (John 17:4–5).

Paul pointed to this same glory in Philippians 3:20–21, writing, "But our citizenship is in heaven. And we eagerly await a Savior from there, the Lord Jesus Christ, who by the power that enables him to bring everything under his control will transform our lowly bodies so that they will be like his glorious body." As citizens of heaven, we are not just waiting to go there. We are waiting for our Savior, our Lord, our King—these were all titles of the Roman Emperor—to come and transform us as he transforms the whole cosmos.[3]

Theologians propose numerous theories about the return of Christ. What do the Scriptures teach us about Christ's Second Coming?

First, Christ will come *personally*. "They will see the Son of Man. . ." (Matt. 24:30). Jesus will not send a committee of angels. He himself will come.

Second, Christ will come *visibly*. "Every eye will see him" (Rev. 1:7).

Third, Jesus will come *powerfully*. "They will see the Son of Man coming in the clouds of the sky with power and great glory" (Matt. 24:30).

Fourth, Jesus will come *victoriously*. "And he will send his angels with a loud trumpet call, and they will gather his elect from the four winds, from one end of the heavens to the other" (Matt. 24:31). He will not come to take sides, but to take over.

The Book of Revelation shows us a picture of our glorious, conquering King. John wrote,

> *I saw heaven standing open and there before me was a white horse whose rider is called Faithful and True. With justice he judges and makes war. His eyes are like blazing fire, and on his head are many crowns. He has a name written on him that no one knows but he himself. He is dressed in a robe dipped in blood and his name is the Word of God. . . . On his robe and on his thigh he has this name written: KING OF KINGS AND LORD OF LORDS (Rev. 19:11–13, 16).*

These magnificent portraits of Christ in these Scriptures provide a hint of our own future. Our Glorious King promises to make our lives glorious for all of eternity and to give us new glorified bodies.

Our Glorified Bodies

Will we know one another in heaven? As a pastor, this is the most common question people ask me about heaven. Their interest signifies more than mere curiosity. People ask because we wonder what we will be like in heaven.

In a world obsessed with makeovers, the original Designer offers the best deal of all. What would we look like if we received a glorious makeover?

The church at Corinth asked many questions about resurrection. In the Greek mind, the idea of a body coming back to life made no sense at all. Remember that the Athenian philosophers abandoned Paul and his preaching over this very issue (Acts 17:16–34). They tracked with Paul's message until he said what God did through Jesus: "For [God] has set a day when he will judge the world with justice by the man he has appointed. He has given proof of this to all men by raising him from the dead" (Acts 17:31). Apparently the concept of resurrection sounded ludicrous and absurd to the Greek intelligentsia.

A few years later, Paul wrote the Corinthians to answer those who doubted the resurrection of Jesus. In this context, Paul passionately proved the necessity of the resurrection to them (1 Cor. 15).

Followers of Christ do not believe in reincarnation, the recycling of souls in new forms. Neither do we believe in annihilation, the idea that death is the end of the story. Much less do Christians claim that we become stars in the sky or even angels. To this day Christ's resurrection remains the foundation of Christianity and explains the uniqueness of the Christian appeal.

Some years ago, I attended a funeral upon the tragic and unexpected death of a child. The family chose to meet in a setting that was nominally but not genuinely Christian in my estimation. Surprised, I noticed that the words in the hymnals had been changed to eliminate any references to the God of the Bible and the miraculous.

Then the speaker stood and eloquently explained that our great hope was that when we looked up on the night sky and saw a star we might remember this precious child. I was disappointed and dismayed. I asked my wife Melanie on the way home, "Is that it?" I understood then what Paul meant when he said, "And if Christ has not been raised, your faith is futile; you are still in your sins. Then those also who have fallen asleep in Christ are lost. If only for this life we have hope in Christ, we are to be pitied more than all men" (1 Cor. 15:17–19). We can be thankful that our hope extends beyond this life into a new life of eternal communion with our heavenly Father.

The resurrection of Christ confirms our hope that we will receive new glorified, glorious bodies in heaven. Paul used the analogy of a seed that is planted and emerges from the ground as a beautiful plant or tree. Our new bodies will be imperishable. "The body that is sown is perishable, it is raised imperishable" (1 Cor. 15:42). Indeed, the body we place in the ground is perishable. Our birth certificates do not come with expiration dates, but death is inevitable.

A few years ago, I said to my wife, "Honey, I am middle-aged." Rolling her eyes, she said, "You will have to live to be ninety to confirm that you are presently middle-aged." Sobering! But our new bodies will be imperishable. This means that they will not degenerate over the ages in heaven.

Of our new glorified bodies Paul wrote, "It is sown in dishonor, it is raised in glory" (1 Cor. 15:43). Despite our best efforts to prepare the bodies of our loved ones, the reality of death is apparent. It is a bit odd to say that a person who has died looks *natural.* No vestige of honor remains in the dead body itself. Yet we are raised in glorious new life. C. S. Lewis placed on the marker of his beloved wife Helen Joy Davidman these words,

> Here the whole world (stars, water, air,
> And field, and forest, as they were
> Reflected in a single mind)
> Like cast off clothes was left behind

In ashes, yet with hope that she,
Re-born from holy poverty,
In Lenten lands, hereafter may
Resume them on her Easter Day.

This is our hope, our confident expectation: that we will all have an Easter day and be raised with glorious bodies. With Paul we will defy death: "Where, O death, is your victory? Where, O death. is your sting?" (1 Cor. 15:55). Paul wrote confidently, "Now we know that if the earthly tent we live in his destroyed, we have a building from God, an eternal house in heaven, not built by human hands" (2 Cor. 5:1).

Nothing here remains new, but everything in heaven does. What if we continue to grow in newness throughout all of eternity? Baptist theologian E. Y. Mullins (1860–1928) wrote,

> There is no reason to suppose that Christian growth will ever cease. At the resurrection, the body will be perfectly sanctified and the spirit at death freed from sin. But as we are partakers of the divine nature and are to be conformed to the image of Christ, the eternal Son, we have an endless vista of growth opening before us. Christ is, as it were, a fleeing goal. We possess him always and yet there will always remain new heights of attainment in him. He ever goes before us to prepare a place for us. [4]

Our new bodies will be raised in power. "It is sown in weakness, it is raised in power" (1 Cor. 15:43). Consider how weak and frail our bodies are here and now. With so many others, I make my way several times a week to lift weights at a club. We live in a culture so obsessed with physical strength that perfectly healthy athletes jeopardize their health to enhance their performance for a short while.

Weakness inevitably accompanies the aging process. Some years ago, after my fortieth birthday, I ran a marathon in Baton Rouge. Afterward, I flew home to Houston and preached on Saturday night and three times on Sunday morning. As I rose to walk up to the pulpit, I painfully felt each stair in the creaking of my knees. My very pursuit of health had weakened my body. I resonate with my pastor friend Ron Lyles, who prayed two thoughts after running a marathon: "Lord, thank you for giving me the health to run a marathon. Lord, forgive me for destroying that health in a single day." We are sown in weakness, but we are raised in power. There is a power beyond the ability to run a mile, lift weights, or hit a baseball. All of our exercise here will not strengthen our bodies there. But the spiritual choices we make do have a lasting impact on our eternity.

Glorified bodies are spiritual bodies. "It is sown a natural body, it is raised a spiritual body" (1 Cor. 15:44). Certainly this means our bodies will be different. We can suppose that our bodies will be like Jesus' body after he was raised from the dead. Remember that Jesus was raised as a body, not just as a spirit. Jesus said, "Look at my hands and my feet. It is I myself! Touch me and see; a ghost does not have flesh and bones, as you see I have" (Luke 24:39). He was able to eat fish with the disciples (Luke 24:42–43). On the other hand, his new body did not bear the limitations ours do. He was able to enter rooms without apparently using the door (John 20:19). Notice, though, that the disciples recognized him and knew it was he.

Will we know each other in heaven? We will know each other so well, we may wonder how well we ever knew each other here because we will "know fully as [we] are fully known" (1 Cor. 13:12).

The coming of eternal life can mean no less than the final defeat of death itself. Death no longer possesses any power over God's people in heaven, raised by the power of Christ's resurrection from the dead. Jesus described it, "Then the righteous will shine like the sun in the kingdom of their Father" (Matt. 13:43). Paul explained, "And we eagerly await a Savior from [heaven], the Lord Jesus Christ, who, by the power that enables him to bring everything under his control will transform our lowly bodies so that they will be like his glorious body" (Phil. 3:20–21).

We are not just waiting to go to heaven, but we are waiting for the Lord of heaven to come to us. When Christ who is our very life appears, we "will appear with him in glory" (Col. 3:4).

A Glorious Place

"How beautiful heaven must be."[5] A good friend sings these words in funeral services. What will make heaven beautiful? More than anything else, the restoration of unhindered access to God will make it all the more glorious. "And I heard a loud voice from the throne saying, 'Now the dwelling of God is with men, and he will live with them. They will be his people and God himself will be with them and be their God'" (Rev. 21:3).

What will it be like to be in the presence of the heavenly Father? In heaven, we will experience unmitigated joy. Why? "He will wipe away every tear from their eyes. There will be no more death or mourning or crying or pain" (Rev. 21:4).

Imagine a world with no more sadness. Early in my childhood my grandmother died of cancer while we lived near her in Rolla, Missouri. I had never heard the word *melanoma* before, but I have never forgotten it since.

After seminary, I returned to Baylor University for my graduate work in New Testament. I left behind a beloved friend and mentor, Virtus Gideon, in Fort Worth. During my first year of doctoral work, I received the message that he had passed away suddenly. The sun must have risen the next day, but I was oblivious to it. Never normally at a loss for words, I found myself spiritually speechless. My wife contemplated how she might bring me out of my despair, but I was inconsolable until that Saturday when we drove to Southwestern Seminary for Dr. Gideon's funeral service. We passed by the long line of gray limousines, climbed the stairs, and walked through the rotunda into Truett auditorium. At the beginning of the service, we began to sing, "Blessed assurance, Jesus is mine."[6] Somehow in the songs we sang and the proclamation of the gospel, God reawakened my soul to the power of the resurrection. My grief had been mixed with guilt, but the presence of our God was great enough to heal both.

In heaven there are no tears, mourning, or crying because there is no more death. The old has passed away, and all has become new.

Heaven will also be a hospitable place. Having grown up in Europe, I remember the closely compacted houses there. The compact cities little resemble the spacious plains of West Texas and Amarillo where I was born. Jesus said, "In my Father's House are many rooms. . ." (John 14:1). One of my good friends and predecessors at Tallowood, Lester Collins, used to say after he baptized, "And still there is room for more." Still there is room for more in heaven as well.

As one of the cosmic consequences of sin, God cursed the ground so it would produce food only through painful toil. Thorns and thistles complicated the work of horticulture (Genesis 3:17–19). As the Apostle Paul described glorification, he spoke of the earth groaning for the glorious revelation of the children of God. Paul wrote of this "groaning" and of "the glorious freedom" that was coming,

> *The creation waits in eager expectation for the sons of God to be revealed. For the creation was subjected to frustration, not by its own choice, but by the will of the one who subjected it, in hope that the creation itself will be liberated from its bondage to decay and brought into the glorious freedom of the children of God. We know that the whole creation has been groaning as in the pains of childbirth right up to the present time (Rom. 8:19–22).*

Even when God subjected the land to a curse, God did so in hope of its ultimate liberation. No wonder John saw not only "a new heaven" but also "a new earth" (Rev. 21:1). Jesus who makes all things new will renew the earth we live in.

Can we truly believe in this glorious place God will provide? C. S. Lewis put it this way, "If I find in myself a desire which no experience in this world can satisfy, the most probable explanation is that I was made for another world."[7]

A Glorious Hope

Today, people attain glory as fame or recognition for some academic accomplishment or athletic achievement. Glory in the Scriptures is better than the best glory of this world because it reflects the radiant outshining of the brightness of God. In this light, Paul said of our own transformation "And we who with unveiled faces all reflect the Lord's glory, are being transformed into his likeness with ever-increasing glory, which comes from the Lord who is the Spirit" (2 Cor. 3:12). Some day that glorious transformation will be complete in heaven. When will it happen?

Every time I read about the deployment of troops to war, my heart goes out to their families. When I was five years old, my father went to Southeast Asia during the Vietnam War. We did not see him for one whole year, and we did not have the benefits of modern computer technology to stay in touch. True, we heard his voice on tape, and we received pictures, but we never saw him.

Then one day, my mother told me that my father was coming home. Elated, I asked, "When will I see him?" She explained that he would arrive during the night and that I would see him in the morning. Knowing our relatives would need the bedrooms, Mom lined me and my brothers up across the living room floor in little pallets.

Somehow I could not sleep soundly because my anticipation overwhelmed me. During the night, I awakened to the sound of a car door closing. I heard the sound of Air Force dress shoes click on the sidewalk. I heard a jingling and then the crunch of the key as it went into the lock. I must have rolled over in time to see the doorknob turn. When the door opened, there stood the broad silhouette of my dad in the yellow porchlight. My father came in, and I saw him face to face. I didn't have to wait until morning. I ran to him then, and for the first time in a year, everything was good. I believe that was just an earthly glimpse of the way glory will be when we see God face to face.

"A Picture of Heaven" is the title of a sermon the great black Baptist preacher John Jasper (1812–1901), pastor of the Sixth Mount Zion Baptist Church of Richmond, Virginia, preached for the funeral of William Ellyson and Mary Barnes.[8] Jasper, formerly a slave, was widely renowned for his preaching ability. William Hatcher, pastor of the Grace Street Baptist Church in Richmond, was a great admirer of Jasper and recorded the sermon in the dialect in which Jasper spoke. Jasper began,

> *Lemme say a word about this William Ellyson. I say it the first and get it off my mind. William Ellyson was no good man—he didn't say he was; he didn't try to be good, and they tell me he die as he live, 'out God and 'out hope in the world. It's a bad tale to tell on 'em, but he fix the story hisself. . . .*

Mary Barnes, though, Jasper continued, "was different. She [was] washed in the blood of the Lamb. . . . Our Sister Mary, good-bye. Your race is run, but your crown is sure."

With his exceptional powers of description and drama, the preacher then picturesquely and eloquently proclaimed,

> *I often ask myself how I'd behave myself if I was to get to heaven. . . . I tell you, believe I'll just do the town—walkin' and runnin' all roun' to see the home which Jesus done built for his people.*
>
> *First of all, I'd go down and see the river of life. . . .*
>
> *After that, I'd turn out and view the beauties of the city—the home of my Father. I'd stroll up them avenues where the children of God dwell and view their mansions. Father Abraham, I'm sure he got a great palace, and Moses, what 'scorted the children of Israel out of bondage . . . he must be powerful set up being such a man as he is; and David . . . I'd like to see his home, and Paul . . . I want to see his mansion. . . .*
>
> *Then I would cut roun' to the back streets and look for the little home where my Saviour's set my mother up. . . . Look there; mighty sweet house, ain't it lovely? Look there; see that on the door; hallelujah, it's John Jasper. . . . Too good for a poor sinner like me, but He built it for me, a turn-key job, and mine forever.*
>
> *Oh, what must it be to be there!*
>
> *And now, friends, if you'll 'scuse me, I'll take a trip to the throne and see the King in his royal garments. Oh, what must it be to be there!*

For certain, "what must it be to be there!" As the old hymn exults,

> O that will be glory for me,
> Glory for me, glory for me,
> When by His grace I shall look on His face,
> That will be glory, be glory for me.[9]

For you, too?

Notes

About This Study

1. Eugene H. Peterson, *The Message : The Bible in Contemporary Language*, Heb. 2:1–3 (Colorado Springs, Colo.: NavPress, 2002).
2. Previous resources available in this series include the following: *Bible Truths About God* by James Semple; *Baptists and Religious Liberty* by William M. Pinson, Jr.; *Jesus Is Lord!* by Howard K. Batson; and *The Bible—You Can Believe It* by James C. Denison. Teaching guides and other teaching resources that accompany these books are also available. The initial book in this series, *Back to Bedrock: Messages on Our Historic Baptist Faith* by Paul W. Powell is no longer in print. See the order form in the final pages of this book.

Chapter One

1. See www.usatoday.com/news/nation/2007-01-02-subway-rescue_x.htm. See www.nytimes.com/2007/01/03/nyregion/03life.html. See www.csmonitor.com/2008/0107/p20s01-ussc.html. All accessed 10/5/09.
2. www.burjdubai.com Accessed 10/5/09.
3. Michael Green, *The Meaning of Salvation* (Vancouver, British Columbia: Regent College Publishing, 1965), 15.
4. Elizabeth Barrett Browning, "Aurora Leigh."
5. Literally Isaiah 50:4–5 says, *God dug out my ear and gave me the ear of a disciple so that I might hear his voice speaking to me.*
6. Remember that Egypt is the same place where God harbored his Son Jesus from Herod's hatred (Matt. 2:13).
7. Hymn text, Frederick W. Faber, "There's a Wideness in God's Mercy," Oratory Hymns, 1854.
8. Lieutenant Iain McConnell as told to Jocelyn C. Green, "A Rescuer's Journal," *Today's Christian* (January/February 2006). See www.christianitytoday.com/tc/peopleoffaith/lifestories/arescuersjournal.html?start=2. Accessed 10/5/09.
9. Michael Green, 29–30.
10. After the Moabites caused the Israelites trouble during the time that they tried to move into the Promised Land, there was antipathy between them. Ruth might have been treated poorly for this reason.

11. See www.ushmm.org/wlc/article.php?lang=en&ModuleId=10005594 and www.pbs.org/wgbh/sugihara/readings/sugihara.html. Both accessed 10/5/09.

12. Vesselin Mitev, "Referee Rejects Compensation for Kidney in Divorce Case," *New York Law Journal* (February 26, 2009). See www.law.com/jsp/nlj/ PubArticleNLJ.jsp?id=1202428602506&slreturn=1&hbxlogin=1. See also http://www.practicalethicsnews.com/practicalethics/2009/02/a-kidney-for-a-heart-some-thoughts-on-ownership-of-biological-material-.html. Both accessed 10/5/09.

13. Michael Green, 31.

14. In Hosea 1:1-9, the decimation of the marital relationship can be traced in the names of the children. These names signify the destruction of the Israelites' relationship with God.

15. "Great Is Thy Faithfulness," words, Thomas O. Chisholm, 1923.

Chapter Two

1. William Temple, *Nature, Man and God* (London: MacMillan, 1934), 401.

2. James Leo Garrett, *Systematic Theology*, volume 1 (North Richland Hills, Texas: BIBAL Press, 2000), 527–528.

3. A. J. Conyers. *A Basic Christian Theology* (Nashville, Tennessee: Broadman and Holman Publishers, 1995), 70–72. *Transgression* comes from the Hebrew *avar* and Greek *parabasis*. *Missing the mark* comes from the Hebrew *chat'a* and the Greek *hamartia*. *Rebellions* comes from the Hebrew *pesha* and *mara*.

4. Garrett, 536–537.

5. Two important lists are found in Romans 1:29-31 and Galatians 5:19-21, listing twenty-one and fifteen sins respectively.

6. Dallas M. Roark, *The Christian Faith* (Grand Rapids, Michigan: Baker Book House, 1969), 217–219.

7. Robert Robinson, text of "Come, Thou Fount of Every Blessing," 1758.

8. Walter T. Conner, *The Gospel of Redemption* (Nashville, Tennessee: Broadman Press, 1945), 1.

9. Bert Dominy, *God's Work of Salvation* (Nashville, Tennessee: Broadman Press, 1986), 21.

10. Dominy, 21.

11. In Roman Catholic theology, mortal sins deprive the soul of grace and lead to damnation while venial sins are more minor, forgivable because not as grave or because done without understanding.

12. "Perspectives," *Newsweek*, January 8, 2001. See www.newsweek.com/id/80626/page/2. Accessed 10/12/09.

13. Stanley J. Grenz, *Theology for the Community of God* (Grand Rapids, Michigan: William B. Eerdmanns, 1994), 199–207. Grenz concludes that the New Testament does not offer strong evidence of inherited guilt.

14. Conyers, 80–83.

15. Garrett, 539. Garrett draws on the work of James S. Stewart to suggest that all of these options may be found in the writings of Paul in Rom.7:25; 5:12–21; and Eph. 2:2; 6:12. See also James S. Stewart, *A Man in Christ: The Vital Elements of St. Paul's Religion* (New York: Harper, 1935), 106.

16. Garrett, 214–215.

17. Eugene Peterson, *Leadership Magazine*, vol. 9, no. 2.

18. Frances Thompson (1859–1907). Thompson was an opium addict who ran from God but found God inescapable. See www.cs.drexel.edu/˜gbrandal/ Illum_html/hound.html. Accessed 10/12/09.

19. I am indebted to a conversation with a friend and attorney in our church, Dale Jefferson, who sees the legal aspects of this dialogue and notes that this is the first example of hearsay as evidence. Neither the woman nor Satan knew exactly what God said to Adam because they were not there. Adam initially evaded God's questions. No one took responsibility, but God pronounced judgment, nevertheless.

20. See www.literature.org/authors/carroll-lewis/through-the-looking-glass/ chapter-06.html. Accessed 10/12/09.

21. Roark, 217.

22. Tim Keller, *The Reason for God* (New York: Dutton Press), 73. He attributes the thought to Rebecca Pippert, *Hope Has Its Reasons* (New York: Harper, 1990).

23. John Calvin, *The Institutes of Religion*, the Library of Christian Classics, edited by John T. McNeill Book 1; Chapter 11; Section 8, 108.

24. I am not unaware of biological research into the subject of genetic propensity toward homosexuality. Although these results remain indeterminate, the scriptural approach of responsibility to avoid sinful behavior remains. For an excellent study, see Howard K. Batson, *The Relevance of Romans 1 for the Nature/Nurture Debate Regarding Homosexuality* (Ann Arbor, MI: UMI, 1995).

25. Alexander Solzhenitsyn, *The Gulag Archipelago 1918–1956* (New York: HarperCollins Publishers, 2002), 75. Google *The Gulag Archipelago* at www.books.google.com. Accessed 10/12/09.

26. Richard B. Hays, *The Moral Vision of the New Testament* (San Francisco: HarperSanFrancisco, 1996), 385–386.

27. See www.twainquotes.com/Blush.html. Accessed 10/12/09.

28. Hays, 210.

29. Dallas Willard, *The Great Omission* (San Francisco, Harper Publishers, 2006), 83.

30. Grenz, 211.

31. Dominy, 24.

32. Conner, 24.

33. Garrett, 558.

34. Dominy, 23.

35. Grenz, 207.

Chapter Three

1. http://blogs.usatoday.com/ondeadline/2009/06/oregon-man-recovers-lost-wallet-after-63-years-.html. Accessed 10/16/09.
2. Michael Green, *The Meaning of Salvation* (Vancouver, British Columbia: The Regent College Publishing Company, 1965), 11–33. Green mentions a fifth word, *kopher*, as well. Each of these words demonstrates different dimensions of God's saving work in our world.
3. Dallas Willard, *The Spirit of the Disciplines* (San Francisco: Harper and Row, 1988), 33.
4. Walter Thomas Conner, *The Gospel of Redemption* (Nashville, Tennessee: Broadman Press, 1945), 52–54.
5. Conner, 57.
6. Conner, 57.
7. Stanley Grenz, *Theology for the Community of God* (Grand Rapids, Michigan: William B. Eerdmans Publishing Company, 1994), 454.
8. Grenz, 452–453.
9. I. Howard Marshall, *New Testament Theology* (Downers Grove, Illinois: Intervarsity Press, 2004), 332.
10. Marshall, 332.
11. Marshall, 333–334.
12. N. T. Wright, *Justification: God's Plan and Paul's Vision* (Downers Grove, Illinois: IVP Academic, 2009), 59–62.
13. Historically the Idumeans were the later representation of the Edomites, who descended from Esau in the Old Testament. Here is the irony: a descendant of Esau was ruling over the descendants of Jacob.
14. The *Magi*—from the Greek word *magoi*—were students of the stars. The text does not call them kings or give them names. Neither do we know whether there were three of them. We do know they brought three gifts that were worthy of a king: gold, frankincense, and myrrh (Matt. 2:1–12).
15. John Ortberg, *God Is Closer than You Think* (Grand Rapids, Michigan: Zondervan, 2005), 103–104. See "Saint Damien of Molokai." *Encyclopædia Britannica.* 2009. Encyclopædia Britannica Online. <http://www.britannica.com/EBchecked/topic/150532/Father-Damien>. Accessed 10/16/09. See also http://www.nps.gov/archive/kala/docs/damien.htm . Accessed 10/19/09.
16. Conner, 87–89
17. Early tradition marks the spot at the church of the Holy Sepulchre as the more likely site of the crucifixion and resurrection. Surrounded by city today, any semblance of the original topography with a hill called *the skull* has been leveled. Gordon's Calvary certainly looks the part with a hillside and rock formations shaped like a skull. In the same complex is a first-century tomb that matches our perception of the description of Joseph of Arimathea's tomb.

18. I am indebted to Josh Guajardo, my friend and fellow pastor, for this vignette.
19. Conner, 112–117. See also James Leo Garrett, *Systematic Theology*, vol. 2 (North Richland Hills, Texas: BIBAL Press, 2000), 53–57.
20. Conner, 120.
21. Hiroo Onoda, *No Surrender: My Thirty-Year War* (Annapolis, Maryland: Naval Institute Press, 1999).
22. John R. W. Stott, *The Cross of Christ* (Downer's Grove, Illinois: InterVarsity Press, 1986), 138.
23. For a helpful discussion of Jesus' self-identification with the Servant see N. T. Wright, *Jesus and the Victory of God* (Minneapolis: Fortress Press, 1996), 589–603.
24. Stott, 151.
25. Stott, 151.
26. "Rock of Ages, Cleft for Me," words, Augustus Toplady (1740–1778).
27. Conner, 112–113; Garrett, 56–57. Garret analyzes the weaknesses of the ransom theory, including its focus on deceiving the devil and its over-analysis of the figurative function of the term *ransom*. God did not purchase salvation from the devil with the blood of Christ.
28. Scholars differ on the precise story of Hosea and Gomer. Did Hosea know she was an immoral woman before they married, or did he discover it in the course of the marriage? I have stated it as the text does.
29. "Free from the Law," Philip P. Bliss, 1873.
30. For a summary, see A. J. Conyers, *A Basic Christian Theology* (Nashville: Broadman and Holman Publishers, 1989), 115–116. Peter Abelard (1079–1142) was the earliest proponent for the *moral example* theory.
31. N. T. Wright, *Simply Christian* (San Francisco: Harper, 2006), 91.
32. "Must Jesus Bear the Cross Alone," words, Thomas Shepherd (1665–1739).
33. My friend and fellow servant at Tallowood Baptist Church, Dr. David Hunsicker, served as a U. S. Navy chaplain for many years. Whenever we talk about discipleship, he comes and whispers the German word *nachfolge*, which means *to follow after*. Christ calls us to follow in his steps.
34. John Donne, Holy Sonnet X.
35. "It Is Well with My Soul," words, Philip P. Bliss (1838–1876).
36. "Amazing Grace!" words, John Newton (1725–1807).

Chapter Four

1. James Leo Garrett, *Systematic Theology*, vol. 2 (North Richland Hills, Texas: BIBAL Press, 2000), 278.
2. Walter T. Conner, *The Gospel of Redemption* (Nashville, Tennessee: Broadman Press, 1945), 140–141.
3. Calvin Miller, *The Singer* (Madison, Wisconsin: Intervarsity Press, 1975), 45.

4. C. S. Lewis, *Surprised by Joy: The Shape of My Early Life* (New York: Harcourt, 1955), 228.

5. Stanley J. Grenz, *Theology for the Community of God* (Grand Rapids, Michigan: William B. Eerdmans Publishing Company, 2000), 407. Grenz explains the etymological development of *metanoeo* from the literal *to know after*, to a change of opinion resulting from this knowledge to a sense of regret and finally to a deep resolve to make different choices.

6. Conner, 197.

7. Although the words belief and faith are not etymologically related in English, they are related in Greek with the noun *pistis* and the verb *pisteuo*.

8. Grenz, 408.

9. William E. Hull, *The Christian Experience of Salvation* (Nashville, Tennessee: Broadman Press, 1987), 33.

10. Grenz, 408–409.

11. N. T. Wright, *Simply Christian* (San Francisco: HarperSanFranscisco, 2006), 202.

12. Christopher Wright, *Salvation Belongs to Our God* (Downer's Grove, Illinois: IVPAcademic, 2008), 163–165.

13. For more analysis of these confessions of faith, consult my unpublished dissertation *Responses to the Light: Sight and Blindness in the Characters of the Fourth Gospel*, Baylor University, 1991.

14. David Barrett, *World Christian Encyclopedia: A Comparative Survey of Churches and Religions in the Modern World* (New York: Oxford University Press, 2001).

Chapter Five

1. W. T. Conner, *The Gospel of Redemption* (Nashville, Tennessee: Broadman Press, 1945), 174.

2. Bert Dominy, *God's Work of Salvation* (Nashville, Tennessee, Broadman Press, 1986), 130.

3. James Leo Garrett, *Systematic Theology: Biblical, Historical and Evangelical*, vol. 2 (North Richland Hills, Texas: BIBAL Press, 2001), 286–287.

4. The phrase "works of the law" has engendered debate among New Testament theologians. Historically "works of the law" has been seen as *the works people do to fulfill the law*. Another interpretation is *the works that the law performs*. The function of the law in Paul's theology can be studied further in the works of E. P. Sanders, J.D.G. Dunn, Hans Huebner, and Heikki Raisanen, among others.

5. N. T. Wright, *Justification* (Downer's Grove, Illinois: IVPAcademic, 2009), 250–251.

6. Victor Hugo, *Les Miserables,* vol. I, chapter XII. See www.quotesandpoem.com/literature/literaryworks/Hugo/Les_Miserables_--_Volume_I._-_Fantine./27. Accessed 10/19/09.

7. G. K. Chesterton, *Orthodoxy* (Whitefish, Montana: Kessinger Publishing, 2004, reprint), 59. Google G.K. Chesterton, *Orthodoxy*, at www.google.com/books. Accessed 10/30/09.
8. Tim Keller in a sermon at Redeemer Presbyterian church, New York, New York.
9. Philip Yancey, *What's So Amazing About Grace?* (Grand Rapids, Michigan: Zondervan Publishing House, 1997), 37–38.

Chapter Six

1. E. Y. Mullins, *The Christian Religion in Its Doctrinal Expression* (Philadelphia: Roger Williams Press, 1917), 417.
2. W. T. Conner, *The Gospel of Redemption* (Nashville, Tennessee, Broadman Press, 1945), 258. Conner contends that the prevailing usage of sanctification and its cognates in the New Testament is for the initiation, not the development, of the Christian life.
3. A. J. Conyers, *A Basic Christian Theology* (Nashville, Tennessee: Broadman and Holman Publishers, 1995), 144.
4. Stanley J. Grenz, *Theology for the Community of God* (Grand Rapids, Michigan: William B. Eerdmans Publishing Company, 2000), 442–443.
5. James Leo Garrett, Jr., *Systematic Theology: Biblical, Historical and Evangelical*, Volume 2 (North Richland Hills, Texas: BIBAL Press, 2001), 402.
6. William E. Hull, *The Christian Experience of Salvation* (Nashville, Tennessee: Broadman Press, 1987), 137–138.
7. "L.A. County tries for 'cuss-free week,'" *USA TODAY*, March 1, 2009. See http://www.usatoday.com/news/offbeat/2009-03-01-lacounty_N.htm. Accessed 10/20/09.
8. C. S. Lewis, *Mere Christianity* (New York: HarperCollins, 2001), 134.
9. Conner, 260–262.
10. John Ortberg, from a sermon titled, "Spiritual Growth: My Job or God's," in *Preaching Today Audio Journal*.
11. "Take Time to Be Holy," words, William B. Longstaff (1882).
12. Conner, 265.
13. Søren Kierkegaard, ed. and trans. by Alastair Haney, *Papers and Journals: A Selection* (New York: Penguin Classics, 1996; reprint), 295. Google Søren Kierkegaard, *Papers and Journals*, at www.google.com/books. Accessed 10/30/09.

Chapter Seven

1. Anne Lamott, *Traveling Mercies* (New York: Anchor Press, 1999), 55.
2. See Epistle LXXIII. 7. www.ccel.org/ccel/schaff/anf05.iv.iv.lxxiii.html. Accessed 10/20/09.

3. William Temple, Archbishop of Canterbury, from a 1944 BBC Broadcast later transcribed in *Anglican Digest.*

4. Walter T. Conner, *The Gospel of Redemption* (Nashville Tennessee: Broadman Press, 1945), 277.

5. Although we cannot be sure, it is likely that Paul wrote before the four Gospels were written.

6. Leo Tolstoy, "Three Hermits." www.online-literature.com/tolstoy/2896/ Accessed 10/22/09.

7. Dallas Willard, *The Spirit of the Disciplines* (San Francisco: Harper, 1988), 258-265.

8. Anne Ortlund, *Up With Worship: How to Quit Playing Church* (Ventura, California: Regal, 1975), 93.

9. Fred Craddock, *Craddock Stories* (Nashville, Tennessee: Abingdon, 2001), 14

10. Lamott, 55.

Chapter Eight

1. Quote commonly attributed to Francis of Assisi.

2. Abraham Kuyper, "Sphere Sovereignty," in James D. Bratt, ed., *Abraham Kuyper, A Centennial Reader* (Grand Rapids, Michigan: Eerdmans, 1998), 488.

3. E. Stanley Jones, *Abundant Living* (New York: Abingdon-Cokesbury Press, 1942), 183.

4. "Redeemed," Fannie J. Crosby (1882).

5. Stuart Briscoe in a sermon at Elmbrook Church in Wisconsin.

6. See www.christianhistorytimeline.com/DAILYF/2002/03/ daily-03-27-2002.shtml. Accessed 11/23/09.

Chapter Nine

1. James Leo Garrett, *Systematic Theology: Biblical, Historical and Exegetical,* vol. 2, (North Richland Hills, Texas: BIBAL Press, 2001), 367.

2. The Greek word translated "assurance" is *plerophoria.* It means *full assurance* or *entire confidence.*

3. William W. Stevens, *Doctrines of the Christian Religion* (Nashville, Tennessee: Broadman Press, 1967), 258.

4. See www.nytimes.com/2009/01/16/nyregion/ 16crash.html?_r=1&ref=nyregion. Accessed 10/23/09.

5. Hymn by George Matheson, 1882.

6. David Garland, *1 Corinthians* (Grand Rapids, Michigan: Baker Academic, 2003), 119-121. Garland states that the one who is saved by fire will enter eternal life "smelling of smoke," his work destroyed. Paul's warning here is real.

7. Michael Green, *The Meaning of Salvation* (Vancouver, British Columbia: Regent College Publishing, 1965), 231.

8. William E. Hull, *The Christian Experience of Salvation* (Nashville, Tennessee: Broadman Press, 1987), 142–143.

9. Garrett, 467.

10. Stevens, 264.

11. Walter Thomas Conner, *The Gospel of Redemption* (Nashville, Tennessee: Broadman Press, 1945), 256.

12. F. F. Bruce, *The Epistle to the Hebrews* (Grand Rapids, Michigan: William B. Eerdmans, 1964), 122–123. With Bruce, I find the hypothetical dismissal of the argument unsatisfactory. Writers of Scripture do not typically set up straw men.

13. Philip E. Hughes, *A Commentary on the Epistle to the Hebrews* (Grand Rapids, Michigan: William B. Eerdmans, 1977), 220–222.

14. "Blessed Assurance, Jesus Is Mine," words, Fanny J. Crosby (1873).

Chapter Ten

1. Geoffrey W. Bromiley, Gerhard Kittel, and Gerhard Friedrich, *Theological Dictionary of the New Testament* (Grand Rapids, Michigan: William B. Eerdmans, 1985), 178–179.

2. Bromiley, 178.

3. N. T. Wright, *Surprised by Hope* (New York, New York: Harper Collins, Publishers, 2008), 100–101.

4. E. Y. Mullins, *The Christian Religion in Its Doctrinal Expression* (Valley Forge, Pennsylvania: The Judson Press, 1917), 422–423.

5. "How Beautiful Heaven Must Be," words, Mrs. A. S. Bridgewater.

6. "Blessed Assurance, Jesus Is Mine," words, Fanny J. Crosby (1873).

7. C. S. Lewis, *Mere Christianity* (New York: HarperCollins, 2001), 136–137.

8. Clyde E. Fant, Jr., and William M. Pinson, Jr., *20 Centuries of Great Preaching*, volume IV (Waco, Texas: Word Books, Publisher, 1971), 227–239. The sermon printed in *20 Centuries of Great Preaching* is in dialect, the form in which it was recorded. See William E. Hatcher, *John Jasper*, 3rd ed. (New York: Fleming H. Revell Company, 1908), 174–183, digital edition at www.google.com/books. Accessed 11/30/09. See also www.blackpast.org/?q=aah/jasper-john-j-1812-1901 and http://findarticles.com/p/articles/mi_m0NXG/is_3_42/ai_n24927505/?tag=content;col. Both accessed 11/30/09.

9. "O That Will Be Glory," words, Charles H. Gabriel (1900).

How to Order More Study Materials

It's easy! Just fill in the following information. For additional Bible study materials, see www.baptistwaypress.org or get a complete order form of available materials by calling 1–866–249–1799 or e-mailing baptistway@bgct.org.

Title of item	Price	Quantity	Cost
This Study:			
This Magnificent Salvation (BWP001098)	$7.95	_____	_____
This Magnificent Salvation: Teaching Guide (available free at www.baptistwaypress.org)			
This Magnificent Salvation: PowerPoint® Presentation (available free at www.baptistwaypress.org)			
Additional Baptist Beliefs and Heritage studies			
Baptists and Religious Liberty (BWP001028)	$6.95	_____	_____
Baptists and Religious Liberty—Large Print (BWP001059)	$8.95	_____	_____
Baptists and Religious Liberty: Teaching Guide (BWP001029)	$1.95	_____	_____
Baptists and Religious Liberty: PowerPoint® CD (BWP001030)	$1.95	_____	_____
Los Bautistas y la Libertad de Religión (BWP001063)	$6.95	_____	_____
Los Bautistas y la Libertad de Religión—Guía de Enseñanza (available free at www.baptistwaypress.org)			
Bible Truths About God (BWP001074)	$6.95	_____	_____
Bible Truths About God: Teaching Guide (BWP001075)	$2.95	_____	_____
Bible Truths About God: PowerPoint® CD (BWP001076)	$1.95	_____	_____
Jesus Is Lord! (BWP001011)	$5.95	_____	_____
Jesus Is Lord!—Teaching Guide (BWP001012)	$1.95	_____	_____
The Bible—You Can Believe It (BWP000089)	$4.95	_____	_____
The Bible—You Can Believe It: Teaching Guide (BWP000090)	$1.95	_____	_____
Beliefs Important to Baptists			
Beliefs Important to Baptists—Study Guide (one-volume edition; includes all lessons) (BWP000021)	$2.35	_____	_____
Beliefs Important to Baptists—Teaching Guide (one-volume edition; includes all lessons) (available free at www.baptistwaypress.org)			
Who in the World Are Baptists, Anyway? (one lesson) (BWP000094)	$ .45	_____	_____
Who in the World Are Baptists, Anyway?—Teacher's Edition (BWP000095)	$ .55	_____	_____
Beliefs Important to Baptists: I (four lessons) (BWP000019)	$1.35	_____	_____
Beliefs Important to Baptists: I—Teacher's Edition (BWP000020)	$1.75	_____	_____
Beliefs Important to Baptists: II (four lessons) (BWP000017)	$1.35	_____	_____
Beliefs Important to Baptists: II—Teacher's Edition (BWP000018)	$1.75	_____	_____
Beliefs Important to Baptists: III (four lessons) (BWP000015)	$1.35	_____	_____
Beliefs Important to Baptists: III—Teacher's Edition (BWP000016)	$1.75	_____	_____
For Children			
Let's Explore Baptist Beliefs (BWP000027)	$3.95	_____	_____
Let's Explore Baptist Beliefs—Leader's Guide (BWP000028)	$2.95	_____	_____

Cost of items (Order value) _____
Shipping charges (see chart*) _____
TOTAL _____

| Standard (UPS/Mail) Shipping Charges* ||
Order Value	Shipping charge
$.01–$9.99	$6.50
$10.00–$19.99	$8.00
$20.00–$39.99	$9.00
$40.00–$59.99	$10.00
$60.00–$79.99	$11.00
$80.00–$99.99	$12.00
$100.00–$129.99	$14.00
$130.00–$159.99	$18.00
$160.00–$199.99	$22.00
$200.00–$249.99	$26.00
$250.00–$299.99	$28.00
$300.00–$349.99	$32.00
$350.00–$399.99	$40.00
$400.00–$499.99	$48.00
$500.00–$599.99	$58.00
$600.00–$799.99	$70.00
$800 and above	**

*Plus, applicable taxes for individuals and other taxable entities (not churches) within Texas will be added. Please call 1-866-249-1799 if the exact amount is needed prior to ordering.

**For order values $800.00 and above, please call 1-866-249-1799 or check www.baptistwaypress.org

Please allow three weeks for standard delivery. For express shipping service: Call 1-866-249-1799 for information on additional charges.

YOUR NAME   PHONE

YOUR CHURCH   DATE ORDERED

MAILING ADDRESS

CITY   STATE   ZIP CODE

MAIL this form with your check for the total amount to:

BAPTISTWAY PRESS
Baptist General Convention of Texas
333 North Washington
Dallas, TX 75246–1798

(Make checks to "Baptist Executive Board.")

OR, **FAX** your order anytime to: 214–828–5376, and we will bill you.

OR, **CALL** your order toll-free: 1–866–249–1799
(M-Th 8:30 a.m.–6:00 p.m.; Fri 8:30 a.m.–5:00 p.m. central time),
and we will bill you.

OR, **E-MAIL** your order to our internet e-mail address:
baptistway@bgct.org, and we will bill you.

OR, ORDER **ONLINE** at www.baptistwaypress.org.

We look forward to receiving your order! Thank you!